MY TRUE LIFE STORY OF
RESILIENCE
&
Toughness

Held by Grace:
A Life Rewritten by Faith and Fire.

D.S. Bright

Unless otherwise indicated, Scripture quotations are taken from the New King James Version.

Copyright © 2025 by: D.S. BRIGHT

All Rights Reserved; this book may not be reproduced in whole or in part by any other means without the prior written permission of the Author.

Published & Printed in USA
First Edition Published in May 2025
Work done under the Auspices of:
Life-Bridge Ministries International.

Available: E-Book, Paper-Back and HardCover.
To be available soon in Audio Version and other languages: French, Spanish, German, and Swahili.
For more information, contact:
Life-Bridge Ministries International.
Montreal QC
Tel: +1 (438) 368 5177
Fb Page: Life-Bridge Ministries Intl.

Contents

Dedication 1

Introduction: A Journey of Miracles and Destiny 3

Chapter 1: The Miracle of My Birth 8

Chapter 2: How I Survived Death as a Toddler 16

Chapter 3: My first day of Fasting 25

Chapter 4: God added Me Tenfold For My Fasting 33

Chapter 5: How I Cheated death in Nairobi 41

Chapter 6: How We Started a Church in Nairobi 56

Chapter 7: How I overcame a terrible addiction 73

Chapter 8: I win a writing competition of 500 ink pens. 79

Chapter 9: The Tough BBC Swahili Competition 84

Chapter 10: The miraculous travel to the UK. 93

Chapter 11: My Search for a life Partner 106

Chapter 12: How I met the love of my life 130

Dedication

To the Holy Spirit, the Greatest Mastermind—my ever-present Help, Comforter, and Genius. Without You, I am nothing. Thank You for guiding my every step, strengthening my faith, and orchestrating every detail of my journey. May all glory and honor be Yours forever.

To my beloved wife, Jemima—my God-sent helper and constant pillar of strength. I could not have asked for a better partner in life and ministry. Your unwavering support, prayers, and boundless love continue to be a blessing beyond measure.

To my dear mother, Rebecca—your resilience and sacrificial love have carved pathways for me that words cannot fully express. You endured pain so I could experience purpose, and I am forever grateful for the foundation you laid in my life.

To my spiritual fathers and mentors:

Bishop Grivas Musisi of *Prayer Palace Christian Centre, Kibuye Kampala*—your teachings lit the fire of purpose in me. **Pastor Mondo Mugisha** of *Empowerment Christian Prayer Center, Mutundwe Kampala*—your guidance and spiritual insight have strengthened my walk. **Pastor Solomon Mwesige** of *Good News Church, Bulenga Uganda*—your ministry has stirred deeper faith in me. **Pastor Pius Muiru** of *Maximum Miracle Center, Nairobi Kenya*—your crusades awakened in me the boldness to serve. **Pastor Fofy Ndelo** of *Christ En Action,*

Dedication

Montreal, Canada—your impact on my spiritual life echoes across continents.

And finally, to **Uncle Paul and Aunt Molly**, whom I owe a special debt of gratitude. You planted the seeds of academic discipline and godly values during my most tender years— *Nursery, Primary One,* and *Primary Two*—at **Molly & Paul Primary School Kibuye**, a season that defined my earliest experience of structured education. You were also there at the summit of my secondary school journey, shaping the final chapter of my high school life in *Form Five* and *Form Six* at **Molly and Paul High School Kibuye**. To bring you last in this dedication is not by accident—but a sign of honor and respect for the exceptional impact you made, both at the beginning and towards the end of my academic path. Thank you for being divinely positioned vessels in my life.

May this book be a lasting monument to God's faithfulness and an inspiration to all who read it.

Introduction:
A Journey of Miracles and Destiny

There are moments in life when we stand at the edge of impossibility, staring into the vast unknown, wondering if there is truly a way forward. Some may call it fate, others mere coincidence, but I have come to know these moments for what they truly are—divine interventions, miraculous orchestrations from a God who sees the end from the beginning. My life has been a series of such moments, each more incredible than the last, a tapestry woven with threads of faith, struggle, redemption, and triumph. This is my story. From the very moment of my birth, the odds were stacked against me. My entrance into this world was nothing short of a miracle—a testimony that I was not merely a product of nature but a child destined for something greater. My mother was yet to become a devoted servant of the Lord, called to establish churches, to spread the gospel, and fight spiritual battles unseen by the human eye and little did she know that her greatest testimony would begin with the fight for my very life.

I was not meant to survive. The complications surrounding my birth were enough to silence my cry before it ever reached the air. The doctors were uncertain, and the situation was dire, but my mother—armed with nothing but prayer—stood in

Introduction

defiance of death itself. She called upon the name of the Lord, and heaven answered. I was pulled from the jaws of death, a frail yet living proof that the hand of God was upon me. Thus, my journey began.

"Are not two sparrows sold for a penny? Yet not one of them will fall to the ground outside your Father's care" (Matthew 10:29). If He watches over the smallest of creatures, how much more does He watch over us, His children?

But, the enemy does not easily let go of those whom God has marked. As a toddler, death came for me again. A mysterious illness—a brush with the grave—and once more, the battle waged between life and death. But God had already written my story, and He had not penned an ending in those early days. He had more in store for me, more victories to win, more testimonies to proclaim.

It was during my childhood that I first began to grasp the power of faith. The lessons came in unexpected ways, through moments that tested my resolve. I still remember my first day of fasting—an act that seemed so small at the time yet held a significance I could not comprehend. Hunger gnawed at my stomach, and doubt whispered in my ears, but I pressed on. In return, God poured out blessings beyond my imagination. Tenfold. What I had given in sacrifice, He multiplied, showing me that obedience always yields abundance.

Then came the defining moments that shaped me into the man I was to become. The trials in Nairobi—where I cheated death yet again—were proof that I walked under divine

Introduction

protection. The streets of that city held dangers beyond what the eye could see, yet time and again, I found myself escaping the very grasp of destruction. Why? Because my steps were ordered. Because my life was not my own. Because there was still work to be done. It was in that very city that we started a church, against all odds, with nothing but faith to sustain us. Who plants a church with no resources, no building, and no assurance of tomorrow? Only those who believe that God is enough. And He was. The doors of heaven opened, and what was once a vision turned into a reality—a place where souls found refuge, where the lost were restored, and where miracles were not just stories from the Bible but everyday occurrences.

But, life is not a straight path. It is a winding road, filled with temptations, battles, and personal demons that threaten to consume us. I, too, faced such a war—a terrible addiction that sought to enslave me. The grip was tight, the chains unrelenting, but the power of deliverance is greater than any bondage. I emerged victorious, not by my own strength, but by the grace that had carried me from the very beginning.

Amidst the battles, there were moments of unexpected joy. A simple competition, a reward of 500 ink pens—who knew that such a small victory could set the stage for greater things? That was merely the beginning. The real challenge came when I faced the BBC Swahili competition, a test that demanded not just skill but resilience, confidence, and the ability to stand firm in the face of opposition. It was a defining moment—one

Introduction

that proved I was more than capable, that my voice had value, and that my words carried power.

Then, the miraculous journey to the UK—an experience so surreal it felt like a dream. Everything that could have gone wrong did, every door seemed shut, yet God made a way. It was a battle of faith, of persistence, and standing firm even when all seemed lost. In the end, victory came. Against all odds, I boarded that plane, landed on foreign soil, and walked into the very destiny that had been ordained for me.

However, through all these milestones, through every triumph and trial, there was one search that remained—one longing that could not be ignored. The search for a life partner. It was a journey in itself, filled with heartbreaks, missteps, and lessons that only time could teach. I prayed, I waited, and I trusted. In the end, God, as always, proved faithful. He led me to the love of my life, a woman who was not just a companion, but a divine gift—a testament that waiting on the Lord never leads to disappointment.

Every chapter of my life has been a testament to one unshakable truth: God is real, His power is limitless, and His plans are beyond human understanding. I have walked through the valley of the shadow of death and emerged unscathed. I have faced mountains that seemed immovable, yet they crumbled at the command of faith. I have seen doors slammed shut in my face, only to have God open windows that led to greater heights than I ever imagined.

Introduction

This book is not just my story—it is a declaration. A declaration that miracles still happen. That faith is not in vain. That when God calls you, no force in hell can stop you from fulfilling your purpose.

So, as you turn these pages, I invite you to step into my journey. Walk with me through the miracles, the trials, the victories, and the lessons that have shaped my destiny. Perhaps, in my story, you will find pieces of your own. Perhaps, in these words, you will discover that the same God who walked with me is walking with you.

Because with faith, nothing is impossible. And this—this is only the beginning.

Turn the page. Let the journey begin.

Chapter 1

The Miracle of My Birth

What an extraordinary privilege it is for me to recount the story of my birth—an event so profound that, in many ways, mirrors the miraculous circumstances surrounding the birth of Jesus Christ. It is rare for one to possess knowledge of the intricate details surrounding their entrance into the world, yet I consider it a blessing to narrate this as a foundational chapter of my life's journey. Indeed, from the very beginning, the hand of God was upon me, orchestrating events that defied human understanding. As my namesake, King David, so beautifully expressed in Psalms 22:9:
"But thou art he that took me out of the womb: thou didst make me hope when I was upon my mother's breasts."
Like clockwork, as the ninth month of pregnancy reached its full term, my mother began experiencing the unmistakable pangs of labor. Excitement filled the air as my family eagerly anticipated the arrival of their newest member. My father, taking his role seriously, escorted my mother to the hospital.

The Miracle of My Birth

In those days, it was customary for husbands to accompany their wives to the hospital, ensure they were in the care of medical professionals, and then return home—only to come back the following day, expecting to be greeted by the joyful sight of both mother and newborn, safe and sound. Therefore, following tradition, my father did exactly that, leaving my mother in the hands of the nurses at Mengo Hospital—one of the earliest hospitals in Kampala—fully expecting to return to a successful delivery.

However, the 1980s were a vastly different era from today. Modern technological advancements—such as ultrasound scans to determine a baby's gender or emergency cesarean sections to handle complicated births—were either nonexistent or far less common. Childbirth, in many ways, was a matter of faith, patience, and endurance. Unlike today, where a simple phone call or video chat can instantly provide updates, my father had no choice but to endure a long, anxious night, burdened with questions that had no immediate answers. Would he return to find a healthy baby boy or girl? Would both mother and child be safe and sound? These uncertainties must have tormented him, robbing him of peace as he waited helplessly for dawn to break. He arrived at the hospital early the next morning, eager to meet his newborn child. However, to his utter shock, my mother had not delivered yet.

I can only imagine his confusion and growing anxiety. Why the delay? Was something wrong? Was my mother in danger? Any expectant parent knows the agony of waiting, where every hour feels like an eternity, and fear grips the heart with an unrelenting vice. As a father of four children myself, I intimately understand the turmoil of pacing outside a delivery room, hands clasped in fervent prayer, desperate for good news. The helplessness, the anticipation, the unyielding hope—it is a moment that etches itself permanently into the soul.

Then came the second day. My father returned to the hospital, clinging to hope, only to be met with the same distressing news: my mother still had not given birth. This time, even she was bewildered. Labor pains that should have intensified instead remained sporadic and mild, as though her body had inexplicably decided to delay the inevitable. It was unnatural, unheard of, and deeply unsettling. My father's worry deepened, his thoughts clouded with uncertainty.

Then came the third day. Surely, by now, the long-awaited moment would have arrived. But to his horror, nothing had changed. No baby. No explanation. Only mounting fear.

By this time, despair had begun to creep in. My father, a man who had never been deeply religious, found himself at a crossroads. While my mother had been raised in a devout Catholic household, his own spiritual inclinations had always been lukewarm at best. Though he was nominally Protestant, faith had never played a central role in his life. Yet, as he wandered through the suburbs of Kampala that evening, weighed down by the weight of uncertainty, God had already set a divine encounter in motion.

The Miracle of My Birth

As he walked, he came across a street evangelist—a passionate preacher boldly proclaiming the Gospel to passersby. With conviction, the evangelist declared, "With God, nothing is impossible!" and spoke of a God who intervenes in impossible situations.

Something stirred within my father's heart. Perhaps it was desperation. Perhaps it was curiosity. Perhaps it was the quiet whisper of destiny, calling him to take a leap of faith. Whatever it was, he found himself approaching the preacher, issuing a challenge unlike any other.

"If your God is real," he said, "then let Him prove Himself. If by tomorrow morning, I find my wife holding our newborn baby in her arms, then I will know—beyond all doubt—that He exists, that He hears prayers, and that He alone is God. And if that happens, I will surrender my life to Him."

The evangelist, unwavering in faith, assured him, "Go in peace. Tomorrow, you will find your wife with your child in her arms."

That night, I can only imagine the storm of emotions raging within my father's heart. Did he lie awake, battling skepticism and hope in equal measure? Did a strange peace descend upon him, quieting his doubts and replacing them with a certainty he had never known?

Either way, as he drifted into restless sleep, something beyond human comprehension was already at work. The God of miracles—the same God who had parted the Red Sea, who had shut the mouths of lions for Daniel, and who had raised

Lazarus from the dead—was about to reveal Himself in the most personal way.

Little did my father know that his life was about to change forever. When dawn broke, my father set off for the hospital, his heart pounding with anticipation. The journey must have felt like an eternity, each step a battle between faith and doubt. Time seemed to stretch and contract in peculiar ways—one moment, he felt as though he were racing through the streets, and the next, as if he were trudging through molasses. Yet, amidst the storm of emotions raging within him, an inexplicable peace—perhaps the quiet assurance of the Holy Spirit—enveloped him, steadying his steps and infusing him with courage.

As he arrived at the hospital and entered the ward where my mother lay, his eyes locked onto a sight so powerful it stole his breath away—my mother, radiant with exhaustion and joy, cradling a crying newborn baby. The weight of the moment crashed over him like a tidal wave, leaving him utterly overwhelmed. In an instant, his composure unraveled, and instead of the customary congratulations or inquiries about the arduous delivery, he erupted into jubilant exclamations: "I am saved! I am saved!" The words tumbled from his lips, charged with newfound conviction.

My mother, still dazed from the laborious night and entirely oblivious to the spiritual transaction that had taken place, gazed at him in bewilderment. Why was salvation being proclaimed alongside the announcement of their child's

The Miracle of My Birth

birth? What had transpired in the hours that separated his last visit from this moment?

Gripped by overwhelming gratitude, my father scooped me into his arms, holding me as though I were the very key to unlocking his newfound faith. There, in that hospital room—amid the scent of antiseptics, the soft cries of newborns, and the quiet murmurs of nurses tending to weary mothers—he declared Jesus Christ as his Lord and Savior. His spirit soared, no longer shackled by doubt or uncertainty. The promise he had made in desperation had become the catalyst for his greatest awakening.

Once his excitement ebbed, he eagerly recounted the events of the previous day—the street evangelist, the challenge he had laid before God, and the miraculous fulfillment of his plea. My mother, deeply entrenched in her Catholic beliefs, listened with skepticism. Though she loved and respected her husband, she was not yet ready to abandon the traditions she had held dear since childhood. What neither of them realized was that the seed had been planted, and when God sows a seed, it is only a matter of time before it bears fruit.

Unbeknownst to me, the day of my birth was not just a personal milestone; it was a divine appointment. The very moment I entered the world marked the beginning of my father's spiritual journey—a transformation so profound that it would ripple through our entire family. As I grew older, my mother would often recount this incredible tale, and each passing birthday was not only a celebration of my life but also a reminder of my father's commitment to his faith. The

The Miracle of My Birth

significance of that day never faded—it was the day he met God in a way he never had before.

Years later, after I had completed Primary Seven, I bore only two names: Bright Ssegawa. But one day, my father, now deeply rooted in his faith, received divine instruction. God spoke to him, telling him that the name "David" must be added to mine, for I carried the wisdom and heart of the biblical David, and my life's path would be marked by divine purpose. Though those purposes are too vast to chronicle here, their impact has been undeniable. As the scripture in Jeremiah 1:5 declares,

"Before I formed you in the womb I knew you, before you were born I set you apart."

My existence had been woven into God's grand design long before I took my first breath.

Through my birth, God not only reached my father but also, in time, my mother. Three months later, she, too, surrendered her life to Christ, embracing salvation with the same fervor that had ignited my father's faith. Together, they became devoted ministers of the gospel, carrying the torch of truth and spreading the message of God's unyielding love. My father served tirelessly, his faith never wavering, until October 2006, when the Lord called him home. Yet, the fire he had kindled did not die with him. My mother, steadfast and unwavering, continued to shepherd the ministry—New Jerusalem Ministries—which flourished, its reach extending across Uganda and Kenya.

The Miracle of My Birth

Looking back, I see the undeniable fingerprints of God on every step of my journey. My life stands as living proof that miracles are not relics of the past but present realities—that divine intervention is not mere fantasy but a tangible force shaping destinies. Indeed, God's plans are infinitely greater than we can fathom, and for those who trust in Him, there is no limit to what He can do.

From the very beginning, I was never just another child born into the world—I was a vessel of purpose, a testimony in the making. And if my birth could spark such a transformation, then I know, beyond a shadow of a doubt, that my life was meant for something far greater than I could ever have imagined.

Chapter 2

How I Survived Death as a Toddler

It is crystal clear that the hand of God has always been upon me, shielding and guiding me even in my most fragile years. However, just as the sun casts light, shadows inevitably follow, and the enemy's hand has lurked in the background, seeking to derail my destiny. Preachers often proclaim that when a person is marked for greatness, the devil will stop at nothing to throw obstacles in their path. I can say with unwavering certainty—this is no mere proverb or old wives' tale, but an undeniable truth written into the very fabric of my life. The enemy, ancient in his schemes, has mastered the art of sabotage, sensing the weight of a soul's divine calling before the individual even grasps it. Like a lion prowling in the night, he seeks to devour before the dawn of destiny. Perhaps that is why I have found myself at death's doorstep more times than I can count. Yet, through it all, the Almighty has remained my steadfast protector, dispatching His angels to snatch me from the clutches of doom time and again.

How I Survived Death as a Toddler

One particularly harrowing incident occurred when I was just three years old—an age where innocence knows no bounds, and curiosity is both a gift and a danger. On that fateful day, my mother was engrossed in her daily chores, completely unaware that her adventurous little boy had embarked on an unauthorized expedition. Like a moth drawn to a flame, my fascination with the world beyond our home lured me past the gate and into the unknown.

The outside world was a thrilling spectacle—cars whizzed past with deafening speed, pedestrians bustled about, and the towering signposts loomed like silent giants. Everything was a mystery begging to be unraveled. As the saying goes, curiosity killed the cat, and on that day, it nearly claimed me too.

Oblivious to the dangers lurking ahead, I toddled down a dusty path leading to the main road, a hundred meters away. Each step was filled with innocent excitement, yet beneath that innocence lay a peril far greater than I could comprehend. The main road, a relentless artery of speeding vehicles, was no place for a wandering child. In my youthful ignorance, I waltzed right into the lion's den, stepping onto the tarmac with the reckless abandon only a child could muster.

From across the street, a group of women at a small shop saw the impending disaster unfold. Their casual conversations were abruptly cut short as their eyes widened in horror. A collective gasp filled the air, followed by frantic screams that sent chills down the spine of any onlooker. Drivers, caught off guard, slammed their brakes with such force that the screeching tires pierced through the afternoon air. Time seemed to slow, as if the universe itself held its breath.

In the nick of time, by sheer divine intervention, the women sprang into action, racing toward me with the urgency of a mother hen rescuing her chick from a hovering hawk. Strong hands pulled me to safety, snatching me from the jaws of what could have been an unspeakable tragedy. Meanwhile, my mother remained blissfully unaware that her child had just flirted with death and lived to tell the tale.

What a miracle of divine deliverance! In the blink of an eye, God had sent His angel to intervene. How else could a mere toddler survive such a perilous ordeal unscathed? It was nothing short of a testament to the unfailing love and protection of the Almighty.

But fate, it seemed, was not yet done testing me.

At the tender age of six, I once again found myself at death's doorstep, unaware of the peril that lurked in my path. It was a weekend—a day of leisure and endless possibility. With no school to occupy my restless spirit, I set out on yet another impromptu adventure. Without so much as a word to anyone, I wandered away from home, my destination unknown even to myself.

My wandering feet led me to our family's garden, nestled nearly two kilometers away in a swampy expanse. This communal farmland, shared among several families, was not just a place of cultivation but also a hub for brick-making. The area, usually teeming with life, lay eerily silent that day—a stillness that should have been a warning, but I pressed on, undeterred by the absence of human presence.

The landscape was riddled with trenches—deep, water-filled channels that snaked through the fields like veins of the earth. Some were shallow enough to leap over, but others posed a real danger, especially for a child of my size. Still, my adventurous spirit paid no heed to caution. I weaved through the intricate labyrinth, unaware that with each step, I was moving further away from the safety of home and deeper into unfamiliar terrain.

Then, as fate would have it, my eyes landed on something unusual—a small body of water, barely a meter in diameter. Floating on its surface was a wooden brick mold, bobbing lazily as though inviting me to play. To my childish mind, this was an opportunity too good to pass up.

What harm could there be in pushing the mold beneath the water's surface? It seemed like innocent fun—a mere game to entertain myself. But unbeknownst to me, the still water concealed a deadly secret. This was no ordinary pond—it was a hidden sinkhole, a gaping abyss that plunged at least twenty feet deep.

Blissfully unaware of the lurking danger, I leaned over the water's edge, determined to force the brick mold to sink. But in my youthful folly, I failed to recognize the treacherous ground beneath me. One wrong move, one ill-fated shift of weight, and in an instant, my small body lost balance.

How I Survived Death as a Toddler

Before I could even register what was happening, I plummeted forward—straight into the gaping maw of the sinkhole.

By nature, living beings sink in water. Yet, in a cruel paradox, when life departs from the body, it is but a matter of days before the lifeless form rises, surrendering to the mercy of the currents. As I wrestled with the stubborn grip of the brick mold, determined to force it beneath the surface, fate turned on me with merciless swiftness. In a single misstep, I lost my precarious balance, and before I could even cry out, I was hurled into the sinkhole's abyss at an alarming speed.

A young child, ignorant of the art of swimming, flailing helplessly against the overwhelming force of the water—I was no match for the depths that sought to claim me. Like a lamb led to the slaughter, I was at the mercy of forces far beyond my control. My fate seemed sealed, my days numbered. Had it not been for the divine intervention of the Almighty, my story would have ended there, reduced to nothing more than a bloated corpse floating on the murky surface within days. But thanks be to God, whose mercies are new every morning, He sent His angel to deliver me from the valley of the shadow of death.

As I plummeted deeper into what felt like an endless abyss, something beyond human comprehension occurred—a phenomenon defying the very laws of nature. The powerful downward pull that had gripped me with relentless determination was suddenly reversed. How? I cannot say.

How I Survived Death as a Toddler

However, as though guided by an unseen hand, my body was thrust upward with a force greater than I could fathom. One moment I was sinking into the unknown, the next, I was bursting through the surface, gasping desperately for air.

Drenched, disoriented, and trembling, my hands, driven by sheer survival instinct, latched onto the muddy edge of the sinkhole. With every ounce of strength left in my frail body, I clawed my way out, dragging myself onto solid ground. I collapsed there, heaving, my heart pounding like a war drum inside my tiny chest. The midday sun beat down upon me, its warmth contrasting starkly with the icy terror that still clinging to my bones. My soaked clothes clung to me like a second skin, the water dripping from my body forming tiny rivulets in the dust.

As I sat there, shivering and breathless, the full weight of my foolishness came crashing down on me. How easily could I have perished! How swiftly could the earth have swallowed me whole, leaving nothing but echoes of unanswered questions! My mother would have searched in vain, her cries swallowed by the silence of an unyielding grave. The thought sent a shudder down my spine. I had wandered off in reckless pursuit of adventure, oblivious to the heartache my disappearance would have wrought. Yet, even in my waywardness, God had spared me. That day was more than a close call—it was a divine declaration that my life had a purpose far greater than I could comprehend.

How I Survived Death as a Toddler

However, that was not the last time the hand of God would miraculously snatch me from the brink of disaster.

A year later, as a bright-eyed, ever-curious seven-year-old, I found myself at the heart of yet another perilous ordeal. At the time, I was a pupil at Molly and Paul Primary School in Kibuye, a school that operated like clockwork. Every day, lessons concluded at exactly 1 p.m., and by 2 p.m., I was expected home without fail. But on this particular day, destiny had a different script.

Instead of following my usual path home, I was enticed by the reckless enthusiasm of my peers. A different route, a little detour—what harm could it possibly bring? The lure was irresistible: an adventure to plunder the riches of nature—ripe jackfruit and mangoes, hanging temptingly from trees like golden treasures. Unbeknownst to us, the very trees we sought harbored not only sweet fruit but an unseen menace—a hidden battalion of tiny warriors, ready to defend their fortress with unrelenting vengeance.

The moment of doom arrived swiftly and without warning. As my companions clambered up the trees, hurling stones to dislodge the fruit, a careless strike shattered what we soon realized was no ordinary beehive. In an instant, the air erupted into chaos. A thick, menacing cloud of bees swarmed out in a fury, their collective hum turning into a deafening war cry.

Panic gripped us like a vice. We ran, screamed, and stumbled— our childish glee replaced by sheer terror. The bees were merciless, stinging with reckless abandon, their venom a scorching punishment for our intrusion. Though we suffered their wrath, by God's grace, none of us succumbed to the assault. As the frenzy subsided, I was hit with a chilling realization—I was utterly lost.

The once-familiar surroundings had transformed into a confusing labyrinth of unfamiliar streets and winding paths. My heart pounded as I turned frantically in all directions, each road a mirror of the last, offering no hint of where I was or how to get home. The sun, once high and confident, had begun its slow descent, casting long shadows that deepened my dread.

Meanwhile, at home, my mother's unease grew into sheer panic. By 5 p.m., her worry had reached unbearable heights. There were no mobile phones, no search parties, and no way to track down a missing child. With nowhere else to turn, she sought refuge in the One who never fails. Desperate for divine intervention, she hurried to Kasubi, where a revered servant of God, Pastor Stephen Ssozi (May his soul rest in eternal peace), resided.

The man of God, known for his deep connection with the divine, listened intently as she poured out her distress. Then, with the calm assurance of one who walks closely with the Almighty, he spoke words that defied logic yet rang with undeniable truth:

"Your son is already home."

It was not a wishful hope. It was not a mere prayer. It was a revelation. A declaration of a reality only he could see. And indeed, at that very moment—at the precise second he uttered those words—I stepped into our home, weary, shaken, yet safe.

How I navigated my way through the unfamiliar terrain remains a mystery. To this day, I cannot recall the turns I took, the streets I crossed, or the signs that guided me. It was as though an unseen force had steered me through the labyrinth, placing my feet exactly where they needed to go. When my mother returned, anxious yet holding onto the man of God's words, she found me waiting—just as he had foretold.

Even now, I stand in awe of the One who calls us by name, who watches over us even when we stray. His grace knows no bounds, and His love never fails. Indeed, as it is written, "The Lord directs the steps of the righteous" (Psalm 37:23). If we surrender our hearts to Him, He will always make a way—even when none seems to exist.

Chapter 3

My first day of Fasting

In the Christian faith, particularly among Pentecostals or the born-again believers, fasting is not just a practice of self-denial—it is a powerful spiritual weapon, a key that unlocks divine blessings and draws us closer to God. It is an ancient discipline, one that even Jesus Himself practiced before embarking on His earthly ministry (Matthew 4:2). Through fasting, we affirm that "man shall not live by bread alone, but by every word that proceeds from the mouth of God" (Matthew 4:4).

From a tender age, my heart burned with a passion for God, and I had developed a strong desire to excel both spiritually and academically. By Primary Four, my efforts began to pay off, and I found myself at the top of my class. However, my position would not remain uncontested for long. In the third term by my classmate, Lawrence, a worthy adversary who shared my hunger for success, dethroned me, setting the stage for.

My first day of Fasting

Thus began an academic rivalry that would shape the years ahead.

The battle for the top spot became a predictable cycle. In Primary Five, I reclaimed first place in the first and third terms, while he dominated the second. Our competition became so predictable that it seemed as if the universe itself had decreed that neither of us could reign supreme for two consecutive terms. It was an unspoken rule, a law of nature that I desperately wanted to break.

As we stepped into Primary Six, the pattern loomed over me like a dark cloud. Since I had clinched the top spot in the final term of the previous year, the unwritten script dictated that Lawrence dominated the second. It was as if an invisible force had written our fates—neither of us could hold the top spot for more than one term in a row. I hated that predictable rhythm, and deep within me, a fire burned to break it.

When we entered Primary Six, I knew the pattern would continue. Since I had ended the previous year at the top, it seemed destined that Lawrence would claim the first position. Nevertheless, I wasn't ready to accept that fate. I was determined to break the cycle, to shatter the unspoken rule. If mountains could be moved by faith, then surely this academic cycle could be too. I just needed to find the right strategy.

I turned to my mother, hoping for some wisdom or advice. To my disappointment, she was unconcerned. To her, whether I was first or second didn't matter as long as I performed well. My father, too, seemed indifferent. However, for me, it was

My first day of Fasting

not just about grades—it was about proving myself, about claiming my rightful place as the best in my world.

Then, as if struck by lightning, an idea hit me: what if fasting could be my secret weapon? I had read about great men in the Bible—Moses, Daniel, Elijah, and even Jesus—who fasted and prayed before achieving great victories. If they sought divine strength through fasting, why couldn't I? My young heart swelled with determination. This would be my strategy.

The problem? I had never fasted before.

The thought of going an entire day without food terrified me. Up until that moment, I had never gone more than six hours without eating. But desperate times called for desperate measures, and so, with unwavering resolve, I decided to attempt a twelve-hour fast—from sunrise to sunset.

That morning, I woke up filled with a sense of purpose. I was determined to embark on this sacred journey. The first hour passed smoothly, but as the day wore on, the reality of my decision began to hit. Hunger arrived quickly, and soon, it overstayed its welcome. My stomach grumbled in protest, my head grew light, and instead of focusing on prayer, my thoughts turned to the one thing I was trying to avoid—food. By mid-morning, I wasn't on my knees in fervent prayer as I had envisioned. Instead, I was lying in bed, watching the clock like a hawk, willing the hands to move faster. Each minute seemed like an eternity, and I was caught in a battle between my spiritual ambition and my physical weakness.

My first day of Fasting

Then, the cravings hit. Oh, the cravings! It was as if my body had entered survival mode, suddenly yearning for foods I had never even thought about before. The mere thought of food sent waves of longing through me. I felt like the Israelites in the wilderness, longing for the cucumbers and melons of Egypt, yet despising the manna from heaven (Numbers 11:5-6).

By early afternoon, my resolve was hanging by a thread. My body ached, my energy drained, and my thoughts drifted away from prayer and straight into the kitchen. I began to imagine a grand feast—warm, golden pancakes dripping with honey, steaming plates of rice and beef stew, ice-cold juice sparkling in the sunlight. The thought of it sent waves of longing through me.

As the hunger pangs grew unbearable, I began preparing for my grand feast. One by one, I gathered the snacks and food items I planned to devour once the fast ended. With each item I placed on my table, my excitement grew, and I counted down the hours.

By 4 PM, I was a mere shadow of myself—weak, weary, and completely fixated on the approaching moment of relief. I had abandoned all pretense of prayer and sat at my table, eyeing my food like a soldier preparing for battle. My gaze flickered between the clock and my meal, my patience stretched thin.

The final hour was sheer torture. My body had surrendered, and all that remained was a desperate wait for the clock to strike six. Ten minutes before the hour, I took my position at

My first day of Fasting

the table, like a sprinter at the starting line, ready to charge toward the finish. My hands trembled as I reached for a pancake, my eyes locked on the second hand of the clock.
Tick. Tock. Tick. Tock.
As the final seconds ticked away, I held my breath, counting down with the precision of a timekeeper.
Three... two... one...
The moment the minute hand touched twelve and the hour hand stood proudly at six, I devoured the pancake in one triumphant bite! Oh, the sheer joy of that moment! I felt like a warrior who had conquered the fiercest battle, like a sprinter crossing the finish line with arms raised in victory. In my mind, I had already won. My hunger had been sacrificed, my patience tested, and my victory secured.
I believed with all my heart that this fast would break the cycle and secure my position at the top. Strangely, I didn't change anything else about my study routine—no extra hours of study, no new methods—just the fast. That fast became my divine contract with God. If He honored my sacrifice, I would break the pattern and remain number one.
As the term unfolded, I found myself strangely at peace. I no longer obsessed over Lawrence or the competition. The fast had settled everything in my heart. I had done my part, and now, I trusted God to do His.
Nevertheless, life, as it often does, threw an as usual, surrendering the outcome into God's hands.

However, life has a way of throwing unexpected curveballs. Our family faced financial difficulties, and by the end of March that year, things had worsened. My mother made the difficult decision that we would move to the village for the holiday once the exams were over.

The village was my father's ancestral home, a vast stretch of land he had inherited from my late grandfather. It was a place filled with history but abandoned for years. It was foreign world, a stark contrast to us, far removed from the life we knew in town.

When we arrived, a severe drought had gripped the land, and hunger was widespread. It became clear that we would not be returning to the city. The village would now be our home. Our new life was here.

The reality of her words hit me like a thunderclap. Not going back meant I would not return to my school, and my carefully fought battle for the top spot was over. Lawrence would now take over the number one position, uncontested, and I would not even be there to witness it.

Had my fast been in vain? Had my hunger, my prayers, and sacrifice—all been for nothing?

I swallowed my disappointment and accepted my new reality. The village school awaited me. I prepared myself mentally for the village school, ready to start afresh, but God wasn't done surprising and find my footing in a new environment.

But just when I thought the chapter had closed, God had one final surprise for me yet.

My first day of Fasting

Toward the end of the holiday, my father visited us in the village. As he greeted us and settled down, he pulled out my school report. I

I took it with little enthusiasm, my heart barely glanced at it — what did it matter now? But as my eyes fell on the results, my heart skipped a beat.

I had done it. I had broken the cycle.

For the first time in all my years of battling for the top position, I had remained number one for two consecutive terms. It was written in black and white — a testament to the power of prayer and fasting.

I was overwhelmed with joy, gratitude, and disbelief. Although I wasn't in the school to celebrate my victory among my peers, it didn't matter. I had asked, and God had answered. I had believed, and He had delivered. The experience left an indelible mark on my spirit, strengthening my faith in ways I had never imagined.

But I now understood something profound: prayer has the power to shift things supernaturally. It can elevate us, move mountains, and change the course of our lives without our own strength or effort. What I had thought was an impossible pattern to break had been shattered — not by my intelligence, not by my hard work, but by divine intervention.

Yet, the story didn't end there.

When I enrolled in the village school, I was not placed in Primary Six as I had expected. Instead, I was moved directly to Primary Seven!

How did this happen? What was the reason behind this miraculous leap?

That, my friend, is a story too great to fit into these pages. But rest assured, the next chapter will reveal the mystery. Sometimes, what seems like a setback is actually a divine setup for something far greater.

For indeed, "all things work together for good to those who love God, to those who are called according to His purpose" (Romans 8:28).

Chapter 4

God added Me Tenfold For My Fasting

The decision was sealed like a letter sent without a return address—I was not going back to town. The weight of financial struggles had pressed upon us like a millstone around the neck, leaving my mother with no choice but to turn to farming, hoping that the soil, in its kindness, would yield something to sustain us. I had to let go of the familiar classrooms I had known, the teachers who had shaped me, and the friends with whom I had laughed and competed. It was a door shut, locked, and bolted. I was stepping into a new chapter, not by choice but by the invisible hand of circumstance.

The shift was jarring. In town, my school had been a mere kilometer away, close enough that I could rush home for lunch and return in time for afternoon lessons. But here in the village, the nearest school was five long kilometers away—a stretch of dusty paths and rolling terrain that required over an hour of walking each morning. Most pupils in our community relied on old, creaking bicycles, their chains rattling in protest as they pedaled through the winding dusty road, while others, with nothing but sheer determination, braved the journey on foot. We could carry leftover food, at supper the previous night, for our break-time and lunch cold and hard which had been kept in warm ashes at the side of the fire area in the kitchen. This was unlike in the town where we would simply carry some shillings to school to buy the snacks of fried *sumbusas* or *cassava*, *mandazi* or *chapatis*, and a variety more. Life here in the village was not just different; it was extremely crucible, and testing the endurance of all who lived it.

There was no time to dwell on nostalgia. My mother, ever a woman of foresight, saw opportunity where others saw obstacles. Asserting that with my ability to always perform excellently in a town based school, I could still overturn tables in the village school in a higher class, she marched me straight to the headmaster's office with a proposition that would have made lesser hearts quiver. She requested that I be placed directly in Primary Seven—the final class before national exams—bypassing an entire year of study.

The audacity of the request was enough to make the headmaster lean back in his chair, rubbing his chin with skepticism. It was like asking a farmer to plant today and harvest tomorrow. Primary Seven was not for the faint-hearted; it was the stage where years of groundwork culminated in one final, defining, countrywide examination.

Skipping a whole year meant I was attempting to scale a mountain in a single bound. The headmaster, seasoned by years of experience, was not one to gamble on reckless ambition.

He shook his head, frowned, and sighed, his eyes darting between my mother and me as if measuring whether determination alone could substitute for preparation. At last, he settled on a compromise—I would have to take a Primary Seven entrance exam. If my abilities matched my mother's confidence, I would be admitted straight into primary Seven. If not, I would settle into Primary Six like any other pupil.

The day of the test arrived, and I took my place before the examination paper. Around me, older, towering boys with deep voices and broad shoulders watched with curiosity, as if a small child had wandered into the battlefield of men. Compared to them, I looked like a sapling among oaks barely twelve years of age. Some of my classmates unlike in the city were already fathers; some of the girls, mothers! Their journey through education had been long and winding, while mine had been swift, yet here we were, about to be measured by the same yardstick.

When the results were announced, the headmaster's skepticism crumbled like a wall of sand against a mighty tide. I had not only passed—I had surpassed every expectation. His doubt was replaced by admiration, and with a firm nod, he granted me admission into Primary Seven. It was settled. I had skipped an entire year and was now in the race towards the final national exams.

The reality of my decision struck like a hammer on an anvil—there was no time to bask in my achievement. I had not just climbed a mountain; I had catapulted myself onto its peak, and now, I had to find my footing before I slipped. While others had spent years preparing, I had mere months to catch up on what they had mastered over time. I could not afford to stumble.

My mother, ever my pillar of strength, left no stone unturned. She sought out parents whose children had previously sat for the national exams, gathering revision materials as though she were storing grain for a long famine. I found myself buried in past papers, notes, and textbooks, each page a battlefield where I fought to reclaim lost time.

Days were consumed by intense lessons at school, and nights—while the village slept under a blanket of silence—were spent under the dim, flickering glow of a lantern. While others surrendered to fatigue, I wrestled with equations, dissected essays, and memorized facts, turning every moment into an opportunity. I knew I was attempting the impossible, but had the impossible not been conquered before by those who refused to yield to it?

The trial by fire was fast approaching—the *mock exams*. These were no ordinary tests; they were the crucible in which students were refined, the storm before the final downpour.

God added Me Tenfold For My Fasting

If there was any doubt about my capabilities, the mocks would either affirm or crush them.

When the results were finally posted, my hands trembled as I traced the list, searching for my name. My eyes landed on the ranking, and my breath hitched.

I was not just among the best—I was the best.

The only student in the entire class to score a first grade.

The one who had dominated before my arrival had slipped into second place, his once unshaken reign overthrown. In a town school, where first grades were common as rain in the wet season, this might not have been extraordinary. But in this village school, where first grades were as rare as snow in the tropics, my performance was nothing short of miraculous. I had not only changed my destiny; I had changed the atmosphere of the entire school. Whispers of awe spread through the village like wildfire. The boy who had arrived out of nowhere had done what was thought impossible. Even the oldest, most seasoned students looked at me with newfound respect, their skepticism giving way to admiration.

Then came the final exams, the moment upon which everything hinged.

I took my seat, heart steady, mind sharpened. The clock ticked, marking the beginning of the test. However, just when I thought I had seen it all, the unthinkable happened.

The invigilator, whose duty was to uphold the integrity of the exam, casually stepped out of the room. A hush fell over the class, the kind of silence that precedes a storm. Moments later, a shadow slipped through the doorway—a stranger, unknown to us yet moving with purpose.

Without hesitation, he began reading out answers.

It was an orchestrated act, one that smelled of premeditated deceit. A ripple of motion swept through the class as heads bent, pens scratched, and students frantically copied the whispered solutions. It was a spectacle—a dance of dishonesty performed in broad daylight.

I sat frozen.

A battle raged within me. Would I follow the herd? Would I discard my toil, my sleepless nights, and my relentless pursuit of excellence, for a handful of stolen answers?

No.

I tightened my grip on my pen, fixed my gaze on the paper, and chose the path of integrity. I had come too far to sell my soul for fleeting ease.

Yet, when the results came, the irony was as glaring as the midday sun.

Despite the whispered answers, my classmates fumbled. It was as though the very hand that had fed them had also betrayed them. Had they misplaced the right answers in the wrong questions? Had divine justice intervened?

One thing was clear—the battle belonged to the Lord, and victory was reserved for those who had prepared in honesty. And as I awaited my own results, one thought echoed in my mind: when God moves, He does not just answer prayers—He gives ten times more than what we ask.

God added Me Tenfold For My Fasting

When the results were finally released, I had passed with flying colors, alongside two others, making us a trio of first-grade achievers. We had set a record that had not been seen in the school for many years. The entire school erupted in celebration, and the administration basked in the newfound glory. Our remarkable performance was credited to the school's improved teaching standards, and soon, more pupils flocked to enroll, eager to be part of this new legacy. Little did they know, it wasn't just about the school—it was about God's divine intervention in my journey.

Because of my outstanding performance, I eagerly applied to Kako Senior Secondary School, which at the time was the crown jewel of Masaka District. Renowned for its academic excellence, Kako S.S. was a school of prestige, attracting top students from across Uganda and the selection process was stiff. It was the dream destination for many aspiring scholars, and I had placed it as my first choice among four schools. The wait for selection was nerve-wracking, but deep inside, I held onto my faith.

Then came the moment of truth—when the results were announced, I had been selected! Kako Senior Secondary School had chosen me! The overwhelming joy that surged through me was beyond words. It was a moment of triumph, a confirmation that God's plans were far greater than my own desires. I had once thought that securing first position in class against Lawrence was the pinnacle of success, but here I was, standing at the gateway to something ten times bigger than what I had initially prayed for!

While my former classmates from Kampala were only beginning their Primary Seven journey, I was already preparing for Form One at one of the best Secondary schools in the region. I was a whole year ahead, walking a path that I had never imagined. Indeed, I had only asked God for victory in a class competition, but He had lifted me beyond that, propelling me into a destiny far greater than I could have ever envisioned. Truly, as the Bible says in Ephesians 3:20,

"Now unto Him who is able to do exceedingly abundantly above all that we ask or think, according to the power that works in us."

This was divine acceleration at its finest, and I was only beginning to understand that when God steps in, He doesn't just answer prayers—He multiplies blessings beyond human comprehension.

Chapter 5

How I Cheated death in Nairobi

Fast forward to the time after my Form Four exams, and I found myself burning with an unwavering desire to serve God. My mother, a faithful servant called to establish churches, had received a divine command to journey to Nairobi for ministry. Without a second thought, I joined her on what would become a life-changing voyage of faith and survival.

Our journey from Kampala to Nairobi was nothing short of miraculous. We had no invitation, no plan for accommodation, and not a single coin for lodging. You might ask, why embark on such a risky venture? The answer was simple: we were driven by the call to evangelize and by the dream of stepping beyond Uganda's borders. Nairobi, often likened to London, had always intrigued me. The thought of experiencing it firsthand filled me with excitement and awe.

At 3 PM, we boarded the Mawingo Bus, a household name in East African travel in those days. We were supposed to arrive early the next morning, but fate had other plans. At 3 AM, deep in the heart of Kenya, the bus broke down. Stranded in the middle of nowhere, we waited in the darkness until daylight, when the mechanics could be summoned to fix the bus. After hours of uncertainty, we were back on the road, finally reaching Nairobi around 1 PM instead of early morning.

The moment we arrived, exhaustion mingled with exhilaration. We had arrived in the fabled city we'd only heard about! With hearts full of wonder, we wandered along Moi Avenue and Tom Mboya Street, soaking in the buzz of the metropolis. On a divine whim, we stumbled upon a church in the middle of an evening service. We joined in, and afterward, my mother introduced us to Bishop Gitari Weru, presenting us as evangelists from Kampala. In a beautiful act of kindness, they welcomed us into their fold, offering us a place to stay—though not in the church itself, but in a hidden residential space behind the curtains, where several male ministers lodged. My mother was offered a place with a female minister, and I stayed at the church.

Bishop Gitari, a tireless servant of God, managed two churches—one in Nairobi, another in Nyeri town—and was working on planting yet another in London. Despite his frequent travels, his vision never wavered, and we were privileged to serve under his leadership.

A month later, my mother returned to Kampala, leaving me behind to continue serving with the ministers. Over time, my

How I Cheated death in Nairobi

Swahili improved, and I even preached in it once—a milestone I'll never forget. But as the months passed, challenges mounted.

With Bishop Gitari in the UK, financial support for the Nairobi church dwindled. The offertories barely covered the essentials, let alone the rent for the entire hall that hosted us. Soon, food rations ran low, and rent piled up, reaching five months' worth. The landlord began threatening eviction. Panic spread, and ministers sought escape before the inevitable closure left us all stranded.

For me, the stakes were higher. I had no relatives in Nairobi. If the church closed, I'd be left to fend for myself on the unforgiving streets. The reality was grim, but we continued to hold services, determined to press on despite the growing despair.

In those moments, I had never been more desperate for divine intervention. Two days before the church was set to close, I decided to attend lunch-hour prayers at another church in the city center. I had long admired Pastor Pius Muiru—his charisma, electrifying miracles, and fiery sermons had earned him great fame in Nairobi. I'd even attended some of his crusades at Uhuru Park, left in awe of the anointing he carried. That fateful day, I skipped our church's service in favor of attending one at Maximum Miracle Centre, unaware that this choice would be a narrow escape for me changing the trajectory of my life. When I arrived, the preacher, a visiting Ugandan pastor named David Mukulu, ministered with an extraordinary anointing. The service was nothing short of electrifying. Afterward, I lingered near the entrance, hoping for a chance to speak with him.

The moment he saw me, he took an immediate liking to me. He asked me to accompany him, unaware that I had no place to stay back in the church downtown. As we walked together, he was greeted like a mighty man of God, and I felt as though the very hand of God had lifted me from the pit and placed me on a hill. At the very moment I faced homelessness, God had carved a path for me. Though I had neither a place to sleep nor fare to return to Kampala, I knew something miraculous had just begun.

That afternoon, Pastor Mukulu enjoyed a lavish lunch, and by sheer providence, I found myself by his side. Eager to serve, I became his armor-bearer, accompanying him around Nairobi, basking in the warmth of the hospitality he received. For the first time, I experienced the grandeur of the city, a world far removed from the simplicity of Ecclesia Ministries, where our meals were often limited to ugali and *sukuma wiki*—occasionally accompanied by a small piece of fried beef. Now, I dined in places I had only dreamed of.

That evening, we retired to Buruburu Phase 2, a well-off neighborhood, at the home of another renowned Ugandan pastor, Apostle Martin Suuna. For the first time since arriving in Nairobi, I slept in comfort, surrounded by fellow Ugandans. It felt like a homecoming, and I stayed with Pastor Mukulu for about a week, savoring divine favor.

How I Cheated death in Nairobi

The very next day, I received devastating news—Ecclesia Ministries had been shut down over unpaid rent! My few belongings had been salvaged by my Maasai friend, who had taught me Swahili. I took what little I had, leaving the rest behind, determined to move on.

My life began to transform. The exhaustion and pallor that had haunted me for months started to fade. Sleeping in comfort, surrounded by divine favor, was a change I hadn't expected. The days with Pastor Mukulu took on a new rhythm—preparing for electrifying lunch-hour services filled with prophecy and the gifts of the Holy Spirit. Afterward, we shopped at high-end boutiques, dined at fine restaurants, and prayed for members in their offices and homes.

Favor seemed to follow Pastor Mukulu everywhere. His love offerings grew so plentiful that he decided to fly back to Kampala instead of taking the long bus ride. Before leaving, he generously paid for my bus fare and asked me to carry some of his belongings, as he was limited in luggage space. In a matter of hours, he was in Kampala, while my bus journey stretched nearly twenty hours.

A week later, we traveled to Kigali, Rwanda. I accompanied him on my first—and so far only—trip to Rwanda. The mission was a success, and we ministered in several churches before returning to Kampala.

But upon my return, Kampala felt unfamiliar. I had no plans, no direction. My heart remained in Nairobi. Anyone who's lived in a major city like London or New York knows the feeling—once you've tasted life in a bustling metropolis, it's hard to settle anywhere else. Nairobi had captivated me. I envisioned my future there, and Kampala no longer seemed to offer any opportunities.

I made up my mind to return. This time, I had no companion, no financial support. It was all on me. I boarded the bus, uncertain of what lay ahead but hopeful. But when I arrived in Buruburu, the warmth I had once known was gone. They allowed me to stay the night, but by morning, I was alone again.

Once more, I found myself facing uncertainty in Nairobi. But deep inside, I knew I wasn't turning back to Kampala.

In desperation, I wandered into Makongeni, where a small church offered me shelter for two nights. But they couldn't feed me or fund my journey back. As hopelessness crept in, I decided to return to Maximum Miracle Centre, attend a service, and ask the pastor's wife for help with transport.

Carrying my few belongings—a worn suitcase with clothes, my Bible, some books, credentials, and a camera from Pastor Mukulu—I resolved to leave Nairobi, defeated. Early that morning, I stored my suitcase at the bus station and headed to the church, determined to plead for help.

A young minister, recognizing me from my time with Pastor Mukulu, warmly welcomed me before the service.

I shared my struggles from the past week, explaining my plan to ask Pastor Lucy Muiru, wife of Pastor Pius Muiru and ministry administrator, for transport back to Uganda. Though she didn't know me, I hoped mentioning Pastor Mukulu's name would help. Moved by my story, the young minister immediately offered assistance, arranging a meeting with Pastor Lucy and promising to provide a place to stay for the night before my journey back to Kampala the next day.

After the service, he kept his word and led me to Pastor Lucy's office. She received me warmly, listening to my predicament. With great compassion, she handed me money for transport and other expenses. Grateful, I thanked her and bid farewell to the team at Odeon Cinema Hall, where the lunch-hour services were held.

Outside, the minister awaited, eager to fulfill his promise. We arranged to meet later that evening to head to his home. True to his word, he arrived on time at a point in the city where we had agreed to meet, and with only my shoulder bag in hand, we set off for Dandora—a place I had never been.

The bus was packed beyond capacity, forcing us to stand in the aisle, gripping metal bars. It was uncomfortable, but I had no choice. We arrived at Dandora Phase 4 around 10 PM, and the minister, papers in hand, led me deeper into the neighborhood.

Suddenly, he turned to me. "This area is risky," he warned. "Let me carry your bag." I trusted him and handed it over, continuing through winding alleyways, growing impatient with each step. When I asked if we were close, he reassured me that we were almost there.

Finally, we stopped at a small kiosk where a woman sold vegetables. "I left my house key with her," he explained. Handing me his papers, he added, "Hold these while I get it." I accepted, seeing it as a sign of trust, but little did I know, I was making a grave mistake.

As he disappeared behind the building, I waited, imagining a warm meal and peaceful rest ahead. It was after 10:30 PM, and the neighborhood was quiet. Minutes passed, turning into what felt like hours. My exhaustion turned to suspicion. Where was he? Desperate, I walked around, hoping to spot him, but he was gone.

Panic set in. I asked nearby residents if they had seen him, but no one knew anything. Stranded in a Kenyan suburb with no money or documents, I was a stranger in a risky area. No one would take me in.

Then, it hit me—I'd been tricked. The papers were decoys, and he had made off with my bag. Desperation gripped me as I wandered from house to house, pleading for shelter, but no one would help.

Lost in the maze of Dandora's blocks, I felt abandoned by God. But in Phase Two, I stumbled upon a large church with "Gospel" in its name. Its doors were open, and with nowhere else to turn, I entered, hoping to sleep on a pew. A small group was praying, and though I was too broken to join, I silently lay on a pew and wept myself to sleep.

Hours later, I awoke freezing and covered in mosquito bites. The prayer warriors were still praying, their voices filling the space. Realizing they were my only hope, I approached them. When they asked for prayer requests, I poured out my heart. They gathered around me, praying for provision, the return of my belongings, and God's divine intervention.

Moved by my story, they pooled together sixty Kenyan shillings—enough for bus fare and a small breakfast. That night, those prayer warriors became my angels. At dawn, by 5:30 AM, I was on the first bus to the city center, determined to attend the morning glory service at Odeon Cinema with Pastor Pius Muiru. The fiery service lifted my weary soul, easing the weight of despair. Little did I know, an unexpected twist awaited.

As the service ended and people filed out, I stood near the entrance, watching the crowd. Then—boom! There he was—the man who had abandoned me the night before, strolling out of the auditorium as if nothing had happened.

Shock hit me like lightning. Without thinking, I grabbed his hand, ready to strike. But before I could react, he smirked and casually asked, "Why did you disappear from where I left you?"

I couldn't believe it. I accused him of stealing from me, but he quickly whisked me away, maneuvering through the crowd to avoid embarrassment. He claimed he was taking me to where he had left my bag.

It felt surreal—like a dream unfolding. Naively, I followed him, gripping his hand tightly as we walked down Latema Road, past Embassy Cinema towards River road. He assured me my bag was nearby, but the lies from the previous night resurfaced. Suspicion gnawed at me. I was certain he was deceiving me, dragging me further from the church.

We reached River Road, heading toward Mawingo bus stage, where I was supposed to board a bus back to Kampala. But the walk stretched on. He kept insisting we were almost there, yet we never arrived. Frustrated, I tightened my grip on his arm, determined not to let him escape, and threatened to drag him back to the church.

After an hour, we reached Pumwani on foot, having walked through Kariokor Market downtown. Still no sign of my bag. By 10 AM, under pressure, he admitted it was at his house in Dandora—the very place he had abandoned me the night before.

We boarded a bus, and since I had no money, he paid for my fare. To my shock, he pulled out a rare green ten-shilling note—the same note I had kept as a keepsake in my bag. My worst fears were confirmed—he had ransacked my belongings.

The bus rumbled toward Dandora, not so packed beyond capacity as had been the previous night since this was not rush hours. We stood in the aisle, gripping poles for support. We noticed three empty seats at the rear of the bus, and while holding one of his hands tightly, I signaled him to go sit with me there. My body by this time ached so much from the previous night spent shivering on a church pew. He refused to sit near the window on his left hand side, as there was a metal framework hedging one from the staircase to the rear exit. It would hinder him from jumping swiftly out of the bus. This is where my suspicion that he had intentions to jump off the moving bus started. I therefore decided to sit on his right hand-side where I could easily follow him in case he dared the impossible. I was holding onto a man who could easily escape, harm me, or lead me into an even worse trap. My chances of recovering my belongings were slim, but I had no choice but to play along.

As the bus swayed over potholes, he fidgeted, preparing to slip away. I tightened my grip. Passengers shot curious glances. We argued openly.

"Your bag is at home," he said. "You'll get it."

"Is everything still inside?" I asked.

"Yes, everything's there," he assured.

But I had already seen the ten-shilling note. I confronted him. "What a coincidence," I said. "That note looks exactly like the one I had in my bag."

He fell silent, realizing I was onto him.

As we entered Dandora Phase Two, the landscape grew familiar—scattered houses and the chaotic sprawl I had wandered through the night before. The bus rocked violently over potholes. Suddenly, he inched toward the open rear door, his arm tensing as if preparing to break free.

I braced myself. This wasn't over.

I moved with him, but he wasn't signaling for the bus to stop. Instead, he planned to snatch his arm from my grip, jump off the bus, and vanish into the residential area miles from his house in Phase Four. In a split second, he yanked his hand free and staggered toward the door, jumping out of a moving bus through the rear door!

I sprang into action, leaping toward the door. Within seconds, we were both outside, and I was chasing him. The bus tried to stop as passengers looked on in disbelief. Since the fares were paid, no one assumed we were fare-dodgers—it was clear I was chasing my 'prisoner.'

He darted behind the bus but lost his balance as he ran in a semi-circle. I kept pace, forcing cars behind to stop. Midway across the road, as he struggled to regain stability, I seized him again. Furious, I reprimanded him for trying to escape and threatened to call the police if he didn't return my bag. I pleaded with him to take me to his house, insisting that was all I wanted. I lamented how I should already be back in Kampala, but here I was—stranded in Nairobi.

We wandered through the same neighborhoods as the night before, me gripping his waistband tightly. I kept warning him that if he didn't stop stalling, I'd alert the neighborhood. My threats seemed to shake him. Finally, around 2 PM, we reached a gate. He led me inside to his house—a small room on the first floor, accessible by a concrete staircase.

Contrary to his claims the night before that he needed keys from a neighbor, he unlocked the door with keys that were in his possession. We entered unapologetically. A small stool sat by the entrance, and I quickly sat down, demanding my bag. I had no interest in anything else.

Calmly, he suggested I have a cup of tea first. But as he turned to lock the door behind him, my instincts screamed—something was off. I wasn't about to let my guard down.

The room was divided by a pale white curtain. On the other side stood a narrow bed, no more than three feet wide. In one corner, there was a small table and a stove. He moved toward the stove, but I kept pressing—where was my bag?

Then, I saw it.

My Bible lay on a wooden shelf near the bed. A moment later, as he pulled the curtain aside, I saw my empty bag hanging on the wall. Rage surged within me. My belongings were scattered somewhere in that room, and I knew retrieving them wouldn't be easy.

He was planning something—but so was I. One of us had to outmaneuver the other.

He gestured for me to sit on the bed, but I shoved him away, demanding my bag before I raised an alarm. As I moved to sit, he struck.

He seized me by the neck and forced me onto the bed, his grip tightening as he tried to cut off my air.

A surge of energy—something I can't explain—burst through me. I fought back, breaking free from his grip and letting out a piercing scream. Panicked, he froze, unsure what to do.

Seconds later, pounding fists slammed against the door. People outside were shouting, demanding he open up. The pressure mounted. Realizing he had no way out, he unlocked the door, and it flew open as the crowd pushed inside.

He tried to slip through them, but they dragged him back in. I wasted no time—I told them everything: how he had stolen from me, how he had tried to kill me.

Now, justice was in their hands.

The enraged neighbors, hearing my accusations, demanded he reveal where he had hidden my belongings and the money from my bag. They searched every corner of the house. Lifting a mattress, they uncovered my camera wedged between two layers. As more items were found and the questioning intensified, he seized his chance. He slipped through the door and bolted down the stairs. Shouts rang out, urging people to catch him, but he vanished before anyone could react.

Instead of chasing after him, we concentrated on gathering my belongings, carefully identifying each item amid the chaos. Among my possessions, we found a stack of magazines titled *Kuna Nuru Gizani* (Swahili for, There is Light in Darkness), published by Pastor Pius Muiru—evidence he had also stolen from the church, where he had masqueraded as a devoted usher.

Accompanied by a resident as a witness, I returned to Nairobi and met Pastor Lucy Muiru at Odeon Cinema to report what had happened. She was stunned to see me back, expecting that I had already traveled to Kampala. As I shared my ordeal, she listened with deep sympathy, shocked by what I had endured. Without hesitation, she instructed one of the ministers to retrieve all church property from the thief's house. She arranged for another brother from the church to take me in temporarily while they figured out how to best assist me.

During my stay, I joined the evangelism team preaching during the lunch hour in open-air meetings at Jeevanjee Gardens, in the City centre, embracing my calling in Nairobi's bustling streets. The man never returned to the church—until, three months later, I spotted him walking down the street, oblivious to my presence. I trailed him for a while before signaling nearby foot-patrol police officers to arrest him.

Once in custody, I confronted him as he pleaded for forgiveness. However, I chose not to press charges, leaving him in the hands of the police and moving on with my life. From that day forward, I never heard from him again, and I focused on my journey until it was time to return to Kampala for another mission.

Chapter 6

How We Started a Church in Nairobi

Starting a church in a foreign country could have been an effortless endeavor—if only I had been backed by a strong financial foundation. But how does one dare to embark on such a mission with absolutely nothing? How can you establish a ministry in a foreign land without the support of an established ministry back home?

When I returned to Kampala in mid-January of the year 2000, I found myself at a crossroads, engulfed in uncertainty. I was young, untrained, and devoid of any experience in ministry or career development. There was no mentor to steer me in the right direction, yet an unquenchable zeal burned within me—a longing to serve God and shape my destiny. My heart was ignited with a passion for missions, but my academic credentials were painfully lacking. I knew I wanted to go into ministry, yet I had received no formal training to equip me for the journey ahead.

How We Started a Church in Nairobi

My mother, Apostle Rebecca, had already pioneered the establishment of churches in Uganda and had proven herself a faithful servant of God. Her journey of planting the first church in the village was a humbling testament to divine orchestration. It was a path paved with trials, beginning with a heart-wrenching loss—one that God used to propel her into her calling. My mother had to endure the unthinkable; she lost her third-born daughter, who followed after my brother Mark, who comes after me. (I am the firstborn son of my mother, though not with my late father.)

In the first chapter of this book, I recounted how my parents came to Christ when I was born. My younger brother was four, and my mother's only daughter was just one and a half years old. It was during this season that God began speaking to my mother, instructing her to return to her ancestral home in Villa-Maria to establish a church. At that time, she had only been in salvation for five years—hardly enough, one would think, to be entrusted with an assignment of such magnitude! Imagine the enormity of the task: A woman steeped in religious tradition for most of her life, now barely five years into the faith, was being called to carry out a mission fit for spiritual generals!

God spoke to her repeatedly through dreams and visions, yet she hesitated. She, like Moses before Pharaoh, offered excuses. Moses claimed he was a stammerer, and in response, God appointed Aaron as his spokesman. No excuse, no matter how compelling, can hinder God's purposes. This was true for

Jeremiah, who protested that he was too young. But God reminded him that before he was even formed in his mother's womb, He had ordained and anointed him for divine service. My mother, however, struggled to accept the call. She clung to city life—the security of a home, a husband, and her children—finding it inconceivable to leave it all behind to camp in a rural village and preach salvation to people entrenched in Catholicism.

From a human perspective, her fears were valid. Returning to her home village, where she was well known, to proclaim the gospel of salvation must have seemed absurd. Would her own people even take her seriously? Wouldn't they dismiss her as a failure who had come back with an outlandish new faith? She must have battled these thoughts constantly, searching for reasons to justify her reluctance.

But when God gives an assignment, He is persistent. When she ignored His voice, He sent others to confirm the message. People—some of whom she barely knew—began showing up with the same divine instruction: "Go to your parents' home in Villa-Maria and start a church." Though she nodded in agreement, she remained anchored in her comfort zone. Then came the final warning.

One day, an elderly woman, well into her eighties, delivered a chilling message. She prophesied God's wrath, declaring that if my mother did not obey, she would lose her youngest and only daughter. My mother received the prophecy with a mixture of fear and awe, yet she still did not move. Then, just days later, my little sister, barely two years old, fell ill with measles. Despite treatment, her condition deteriorated rapidly, and in the span of three days, she succumbed to the illness.

My mother had known, deep down, that this was a divine consequence. When my sister passed on, she did not shed tears, though she mourned deeply. She carried the weight of regret—the bitter realization that her disobedience had cost her something precious. With a heart full of sorrow but a spirit now yielded to God's will, she set off for the village.

What followed was nothing short of a divine outpouring. The first souls to receive Christ were her own parents—staunch Catholics in their seventies who had never wavered in their religious beliefs. Yet when my mother prayed for them, their ailments vanished. Instant healing swept through their household, and in the face of such undeniable power, they abandoned the faith they had clung to all their lives and embraced Christ.

Word spread quickly, and soon the entire village began to experience a spiritual awakening. Lives were transformed, and salvation took root in the unlikeliest of places. The power of the Holy Ghost descended mightily, shaking the very foundations of the village. Among those who came to Christ was my mother's younger brother. Overcome by the zeal of his newfound faith, he immediately stepped into the role of an evangelist.

My grandfather, overjoyed by the move of God, did something extraordinary—he donated an acre of land to build a church. Soon, those who had embraced salvation began to gather in worship, and as the congregation grew, my uncle—the same young brother to my mother who had given his life to Christ—rose to become the pastor of the church.

This was the genesis of a great work in Villa-Maria, Masaka District in Uganda, one that would ripple through generations. My mother's obedience—though delayed—had unlocked a mighty revival in a place where salvation had once been an alien concept. It was a lesson etched deeply into my heart: when God calls, obedience is not just an option—it is a necessity. Sometimes, in fact all times, the price of resistance is far too great to bear.

As I stood on the precipice of my own ministry journey, grappling with uncertainty and lack, my mother's story served as both a cautionary tale and a source of encouragement. If God had moved so powerfully through her obedience, wouldn't He do the same for me if I simply trusted and followed where He led? The road ahead was uncertain, but one thing remained clear—God's call, once given, would not be revoked. And if He had called me, He would surely make a way.

With God, indeed, nothing is impossible. My mother left the village within just a few weeks, but a tremendous work of evangelism had already been accomplished. A great wave of the gospel was shaking the entire village and the neighboring communities, and to this day, the church she planted still stands as a testament to God's faithfulness.

Years later, my mother received her second divine assignment—to plant another church, this time about ten to fifteen kilometers away from the first one. It was during this season that God anointed and ordained her into the office of an apostle. Among the many trials she faced was overcoming fear. At that time, we were living deep in the village, and my late father was pastoring a small church within our homestead. Meanwhile, my mother was being prepared to establish another church approximately forty kilometers away.

Fear, particularly the kind that plagues many women—the fear of darkness, the unknown, and unseen forces—was a stronghold in her life. Nevertheless, God was determined to break this bondage, and the method He chose was both radical and transformative. One night, He instructed her to move her beddings from inside the house to the veranda and sleep outside indefinitely. She was to remain there until God released her.

Our home was surrounded by thick banana plantations, and the village was infamous for night dancers—demonic witches who operated in the cover of darkness. These night witches were known to manipulate the wind, exhume corpses using supernatural forces, and engage in horrifying rituals, including cannibalism. They could clap their hands at night and produce fire, perform dark enchantments, and terrorize the village with their eerie presence. No one dared to walk alone at late night in that place. Yet, here was my mother, called to pass through a divine test before being fully commissioned into her apostolic calling.

She obeyed. She set up a makeshift shelter against the rain and wind but was, in essence, sleeping under the open sky, alone.

One fateful night, as she lay in her humble outdoor shelter, a night-witch approached. She felt an overwhelming force engulf her—paralyzing fear gripped her as the sinister presence loomed closer. The terrifying entity had the power to kill and devour human flesh. My mother tried to scream for help but found that she was frozen—her voice stifled, her body unable to move. In her spirit, she cried out to Jesus. Suddenly, she heard a bell ringing in the heavens. In that instant, the witch fled, his dark force shattered by the divine intervention.

She could not explain how she had been saved, but it was a powerful demonstration of God's deliverance. This ordeal repeated itself several times until she no longer feared the night dancers. Eventually, she grew bold enough to confront them directly, knowing that the power of God was always available to rescue her.

For us, her children, this experience was a life-altering lesson in faith. It proved that no power of darkness could stand against those who trust in the Lord. After a season of testing, God instructed her to return her bedding to the house. The fear that once controlled her was gone. She had graduated in the Spirit, and now, anointed and emboldened, she was ready to establish the new church.

Miracles of provision followed. The church grew rapidly as many surrendered their lives to Christ. A place was provided for the congregation, and soon, a thriving fellowship was established. She dedicated herself fully to the work, staying there for two weeks at a time and returning home for only three days in between.

The journey between our home and the new church was grueling. The forty-kilometer distance was not easily accessible by any reliable means of transport. Undeterred, my mother made a bold decision—she would ride a bicycle between the two places! Even then, she battled a new challenge: the fear of how people would perceive a married woman of her age riding a bicycle. To overcome this, she made an extraordinary choice—she would cycle the forty kilometers at night!

For an entire year, until the church was fully established, my mother faithfully rode her bicycle back and forth, twice every two weeks. The church flourished while the stronghold of witchcraft in the village crumbled. Some witches abandoned their evil practices, while others fled the area altogether. Spiritually, my mother had graduated as an apostle, and with this newfound authority, she could now plant churches without fear.

Years later, after I returned from Nairobi, God gave my mother another assignment—this time, to plant her third church in Nairobi. We had previously traveled to Nairobi together about eight months earlier, but she had left me there to face significant trials. Now, it was time for us to return together to fulfill God's mission.

At the time, the season was dry—rains had not fallen for months. But God gave my mother a peculiar sign: "When the rain comes, pack your bags and go to Nairobi." We waited in Kampala for two weeks, watching the sky, our suitcases packed and ready. Then, in the middle of that parched season, an unusual downpour swept through the land. It was the sign we had been waiting for—a miraculous confirmation of God's instruction. Without hesitation, we set off for Nairobi.

Looking back at how God had trained my mother in obedience, it became clear that we could not have stepped into this next mission without the faith she had developed through hardship. Had she not undergone rigorous training—learning to follow God's instructions even when it hurt—we might never have embarked on this journey. Hebrews 5:8 says, "Though He was a Son, yet He learned obedience by the things which He suffered." My mother had also learned obedience through suffering. Now, equipped with unshakable faith, she was ready for the next great move of God.

This was the second time we were traveling together to Nairobi. The first time, we had visited a place called Githurai

How We Started a Church in Nairobi

45, where we stayed at PEFA All Nations Church under the leadership of Pastor Gudoi Wesonga, a Ugandan based in Kenya. He had welcomed us warmly, and my mother had served in the church, praying for many sick people who miraculously experienced God's healing power. The church members had shown us exceptional hospitality, and one of the church elders, Mr. Kabao had even hosted us in his home. Now, returning for a second time with the divine instruction to plant a church, we thought of approaching Pastor Wesonga, believing that since our mission was God-ordained, it would be received with open arms. However, we were about to face unexpected opposition.

At the time of writing this book, twenty-three years have passed since these events, yet they remain as clear in my mind as though they happened yesterday. It was undoubtedly the hand of God that carried us through it all. The heavy rain, our sign to set off, came on a Thursday afternoon, and by Friday afternoon, we were on a bus to Nairobi. We arrived in the city on Saturday afternoon and went straight to Githurai 45, to the home of the elder who had previously hosted us.

To our surprise, he and his wife were not expecting us, and their reaction made it clear that our presence was unwelcome. The wife frowned upon seeing us, and later that evening, when the husband returned from work, we sat anxiously in the room they had given us, wondering what would become of us. We had little money—barely enough to rent a single room in Githurai. Before supper, the couple called us to their living room and asked about the purpose of our return to Nairobi. When we explained that God had sent us to start a church and that we were under divine command, they openly opposed the idea and made it clear that they would not accommodate us.

The following morning was Sunday. The church elder left early for the PEFA church, while we followed later, hoping that Pastor Wesonga would have a different opinion and allow us to appeal to him regarding God's instructions. However, upon arrival, we discovered that the elder had already briefed him about our intentions. A guard had been stationed at the entrance to prevent us from entering. We could not even see the pastor, who was actively working to frustrate our mission. The situation had gone from bad to worse.

We could not return to the elder's house to collect our belongings, as we had nowhere to stay. With no money to rent even the cheapest single room, we wandered around Githurai until we found and settled down at a solitary place with green grass and shade near a thicket on the outskirts of that neighbourhood. We engaged in fasting and prayer, until late evening. After six o'clock towards dawn, we decided to walk back to the elder's house, unsure of what awaited us. We feared that our belongings had already been thrown out and that we would be left stranded.

As we walked along the patched mucky and crowded stretch between PEFA Church at Kimbo and the elder's house, we noticed a rental block of rooms built in a U-shape. The open end of the U without a gate faced the road. The left-hand side had three occupied rooms, while the right-hand side had three unfinished rooms—unplastered, without windows and doors. Near the last room on the roadside, we saw a person sitting by the door. We asked her about the vacant unfinished rooms, and she pointed to the landlord's door, at the extreme right-hand corner inside the U-shaped block.

We approached the house and knocked. A skinny, youthful-looking man answered the door. Introducing ourselves as preachers from Uganda, we explained that God had sent us to start a church. With no money to afford a furnished room, we humbly asked to rent one of the unfinished spaces, offering the only three hundred Kenya shillings we had left.

The landlord glanced at the money and shook his head. It was too little, he said, and an unfinished room—without windows or doors—was not worth renting. Then, in a moment of unexpected kindness, he told us we could stay in one of the empty rooms for free. He stared at us, puzzled, as if wondering how we would even manage to sleep there.

Overjoyed at God's provision, we hurried back to the elder's house to collect our suitcases. Without revealing where we were going, we left, feeling relieved to be out of their home. The unfinished house, though lacking doors or windows, felt more welcoming than a well-furnished home where the hosts had turned hostile. We shielded the room's openings with bed-sheets, laid a simple mat on the floor, and slept in peace.

The following day, we realized we could use the second vacant room for preparing food and the third as a place of worship. Thus began the miraculous journey of planting a church in Nairobi, with nothing but faith and divine guidance. The residents of the three single-roomed houses on the opposite side were generally friendly to us, though the occupant of the middle room was operating a small evening bar, her single room hosting her family of five people and cans of booze while the small space in front of her room in the open space hosted a bunch of drunkards each night till late creating noise and chaos within the homestead. Moreover the small open space between the two rows in that block was untidy, strewn with stones, and would flood with dirty water during the rainy season.

Amidst this challenging environment, we remained steadfast in prayer. Every evening, we would gather in the third room on the right handside to seek God, and on Friday nights, we held all-night prayer vigils. Soon, word spread that we had returned, and those who had previously experienced miracles at the PEFA Church began joining us. More and more people came to pray with us, and before we knew it, two months had passed.

One day, a woman from the neighborhood, suffering from severe health issues, heard about us. She was told that some preachers from Uganda were in the area, and that they could pray for healing. Desperate for a breakthrough, she approached my mother, who prayed for her. Miraculously, she regained her health. Overjoyed, she invited us to visit her home and meet her husband.

Her husband turned out to be a jovial and hospitable man who welcomed us warmly. During our conversation, he shared his burdens—he was a quantity surveyor who had completed several government contracts but had yet to receive the large sums of money owed to him. As my mother led us in prayer, she advised him to sow a financial seed, an act of faith that could hasten the release of his long-overdue payments. He took her words to heart and gave us a thousand Kenyan shillings. At that moment, it felt like a fortune to us, as our usual church offerings ranged between sixty and one hundred and twenty shillings, mostly in coins or a few small paper notes.

That night, as we left their home, we glorified God for such a great blessing. The man also vowed that if the government paid him, he would give us a tithe of the money. We expected this to take at least a month, but to our amazement, we received a call from the wife only three days later summoning us back to the their home for the testimony! The government had contacted him the very next day and released a significant portion of the money owed to him. When he invited us back to his home, we could hardly believe what God had done.

For years, the government had been reluctant to settle his debt, leading Mr. Wangai to consider filing a lawsuit. Yet, within hours of our prayer, what seemed impossible had come to pass. It was a powerful confirmation that God had indeed sent us to Githurai, and He was proving Himself faithful. When we arrived, we found Mr. Wangai beaming with joy, while his wife was busy preparing a celebratory meal for us. He testified that when we prayed, he had asked God for a sign—if the money started coming within a month, he would know it was truly God at work. Yet, in just a matter of hours, the government department responsible had responded and made the first payment!

Even though we had prayed in faith, the speed of God's intervention left us in awe. That night, we worshiped and celebrated the mighty power of God. Before we left, Mr. Wangai pulled out a large envelope and handed it to us in the presence of his wife. It contained ten percent of the amount he had received, as he had promised. He reaffirmed his vow to continue giving us a tithe of every payment that came in. The government had only settled a fragment of his debt whose ten percent alone was many hundreds of thousands of Kenya shillings that we had never dreamt of possessing in just a single night! Many corporations still owed him large sums from past contracts yet, he was determined to honor God by faithfully tithing on every payment.

We were overwhelmed with joy and gratitude. Never had we imagined that in a foreign land, with no resources of our own, God would open such extraordinary doors simply because we had obeyed His call. Returning to our ramshackle home that night with millions in hand, we suddenly felt unsafe. We could barely sleep, not just because of the excitement, but also because of an unusual swarm of mosquitoes that seemed to have invaded our room that very night. For two months, we had lived in that humble space without experiencing a single mosquito bite—yet on this one night, we could barely endure them!

By the break of dawn, we knew it was time to move. That very morning, we searched for a decent house in the neighborhood and relocated the same day. We also rushed to town to purchase mattresses, bedding, and other essentials that we had lacked for the two months we had stayed in the ramshackle. In the following days, we continued furnishing our home, buying furniture and kitchen utensils. The transformation was so sudden that our neighbors marveled at how we had seemingly become wealthy overnight!

A few days later, we were invited back to Mr. Wangai's home for yet another tithe offering from a fresh payment he had received. This time, we made a firm decision to shift the church from the small single-roomed house to a larger, well-furnished rented hall. Our ministry was visibly advancing, and people took notice. Even those from the PEFA Church, who had initially opposed us, could not deny that God was with us. Our progress was a testimony that we were truly sent by God.

Money continued to flow in for a long period, and the work of the Lord flourished in Nairobi. Then, in His divine timing,

God gave us a new assignment, leading us to yet another chapter of faith and obedience.

Chapter 7

How I overcame a terrible addiction

During my time at Ekklesia Ministries, Nairobi, the church where I first stayed with my mother when we went to Kenya for ministry mission, I was so active and enthusiastic to serve. The Church attracted large congregations who gathered to worship and hear the Word of God. One day, an elderly man in his sixties attended a service. He had a handcuffed arm, recovering from a fracture. As the service ended, I greeted him along with other congregants, but he requested that I accompany him to his residence nearby. He was staying in a hotel room on Kirinyaga Road, just a few meters away from the church.

Curious about his background and circumstances, I engaged him in conversation over a shared meal at his place. Later that evening, another young man, who was sharing the room with him, arrived. The room contained two single beds—his was slightly larger than the one in the opposite corner. As night fell, I prepared to return to the church, where I resided.

However, the elderly man insisted that I stay the night. I hesitated, as I had not informed my fellow ministers and mobile phones were not common at the time. Yet, he was persistent, and I eventually relented.

To my discomfort, he directed me to sleep in his bed instead of the empty one. Though I would have preferred to sleep with the younger man, I complied. He then insisted that I remove my dusty clothes, citing the clean white bedsheets as the reason. Unaware of his true intentions, I complied, keeping only my undergarments on. Once we were under the blankets, the lights went out.

Moments later, I felt a hand gently massaging my back. It was his left hand—the only functional one since his right arm was injured and handcuffed. I was in utter shock! I did not know what to do because it was extremely weird and unacceptable for me! I did not know what to do. Slowly, he moved his hand downward toward my underpants, pressing his body closer to mine. At first, I resisted, unsure of what was happening next. But he persisted, his hand forcing its way into my private areas.

I was fortunate that his injured arm prevented him from overpowering me completely. However, he managed to stimulate me against my will, introducing me to a sexual experience I had never known before. That night, I unwillingly encountered masturbation for the first time—something I had neither been exposed to nor understood prior to that moment.

How I overcame a terrible addiction

What followed was a battle I never anticipated. That night's experience triggered a terrible addiction that would haunt me for years. Little did I know that the enemy had sown a seed of bondage that would take the mighty hand of God to uproot. However, through God's grace, I would later overcome it, experiencing the true power of deliverance and restoration.

The following morning, I returned to the church, grateful that God had spared me from a possible homosexual involvement. Little did I know, however, that a different door had been opened—one that led to the vice of masturbation. Soon, a fierce battle against this new temptation began.

A few days later, I found myself longing for the excitement I had felt when the old man touched me. The pleasure was so intense that I couldn't resist it. Yet, along with the pleasure came a deep sense of guilt. In my spirit, I knew it was something that did not please God. I tried to resist, but the urge to masturbate only grew stronger. Another voice whispered justifications: "It's not so bad. After all, I'm not engaging in intercourse with anyone; I'm only quenching my own sexual thirst." There was also the thought that it was safer—no risk of HIV/AIDS since I wasn't with anyone. Yet, despite all these justifications, the guilt never left.

Years passed, and the struggle continued, quietly underlying my ministry. On the outside, everything seemed to be going well. I was preaching, seeing signs, wonders, and miracles. But beneath it all, this secret vice was eating away at my conscience.

How I overcame a terrible addiction

I had been the leading Pastor of this small church my mother, the Apostle, had planted in Githurai, Nairobi, for four years. Despite the success of the ministry, I felt a deep sense of inadequacy. One day, I gathered the courage to confide in my mother, asking her to pray for me. Unfortunately, she didn't know much about deliverance or counseling for such struggles. She prayed for me, and while I felt some relief, there was no complete deliverance as I kept falling back into the same troubles. Upon returning to Kampala, she discussed the matter with my father. They agreed that the time had come for me to find a wife—one way I could be helped to overcome the vice threatening my life and ministry.

My mother cautioned me against marrying a Kenyan woman, fearing that cultural differences would make the marriage too difficult to endure. Around the same time, I met a Ugandan preacher named Gershom, who shared his experience of living in Kenya and marrying a Kikuyu woman he loved dearly. But one day, he returned home to find the house empty. He too warned me against marrying outside my tribe, especially a Kikuyu woman, suggesting that it was best for a Kikuyu man to marry within his own tribe.

With this in mind, I began to consider returning to Uganda to find a wife. My mother, meanwhile, had identified a woman in the church she had started at our home in Kampala. She spoke highly of her, and I eagerly anticipated meeting her upon my return.

When I got to Kampala, I hadn't planned on staying long, but unexpectedly, I found myself settling in. An opportunity arose for me to further my education—Uncle Paul from Molly and Paul Schools offered me a sponsorship to study A-levels at his school in Makindye, Kampala just a kilometre from our home.

I also met the girl my mother had suggested to be my wife, but I wasn't impressed. She was beautiful, but her character didn't align with the image of the woman I envisioned as my future wife. So, I decided to focus on my studies instead.

Yet, even as I concentrated on my education, the vice of masturbation continued to haunt me in silence. Throughout my first year of A-levels, I fasted and prayed daily, desperately seeking deliverance. When I fasted, my body grew weak, and I could resist the temptation. But as soon as I broke my fast and regained strength, the urges would return, along with the guilt. For six years, I had mutely fought this battle without success.

In my seventh year of struggling with the vice, while still at Molly and Paul High School, God sent a pastor whose ministry focused on helping youth. I opened up to him about my struggle, and he offered me much-needed counsel and encouragement. Together, we prayed, and it was then that the powerful force driving me into the vice finally stopped. It was so miraculous that it only required my confession, and surrender to God by letting someone else pray for me.

God's plan for me was to experience firsthand the struggles that many youth face when they are held hostage by destructive vices. I can see now that had it not been for the power of confession and the prayer of repentance, I would have remained trapped in this horrible vice even into marriage.

God is faithful. He knows exactly what we are going through. If you are facing bondage or pain, take heart—God will make a way where there seems to be none. He will deliver you from the grip of the enemy.

Chapter 8

I win a writing competition of 500 ink pens.

When I joined Form Five at Molly and Paul High School, I was known as an excellent student in science subjects, stepping into the advanced secondary level with confidence. Naturally, I had to find a science combination of subjects to pursue. However, the school only offered Arts subjects at A-level, except for Mathematics. For an entire first term, I wrestled with the challenge of crafting my own combination from what was available mixing Mathematics with Divinity! Eventually, I was cautioned that my unconventional subject mix would not be accepted at the university level, let alone for the final exams in Form Six.

. Left with no other option, I decided to pursue a combination that included two subjects out of four, the school did not offer: Physics, a pure science, and French, a language.

Throughout the entire first term, I had no opportunity to study these two subjects, yet I knew I had to excel. By second term, I doubled down on my efforts to catch up with my peers

I win a writing competition of 500 ink pens.

in other schools. I found myself almost entirely alone in these subjects, with no classmates to study alongside. Physics was divided into three demanding segments, while French had four different aspects to master. Despite these challenges, I soldiered on, relying heavily on self-directed research and dedicated personal study.

During my first term at A-level, I discovered a valuable resource—academic papers featuring questions and answers for various classes. I routinely bought these newspapers to supplement my school revision materials. One day, nestled within those same booklets, I stumbled upon an advertisement. A company that produced "Nice Clear" pens had partnered with *New Vision* newspaper to announce a competition. They promised a reward of 500 fine-quality pens to the student who could write the best essay about how they had benefited from the newspaper's revision pullouts. The competition was open to students from Senior One to Six across the country. Entries could be mailed to the *New Vision* offices or delivered directly to their headquarters in Kampala's Industrial Area.

I no longer recall whether I posted my essay or delivered it in person, but I do remember pouring my heart and soul into crafting that piece. The first term came and went, and no word arrived from the *New Vision* team. By the time we returned for second term in June, the competition had faded from my mind. I couldn't imagine I had any chance of winning. After all, I had written my best, but I had no way of comparing my

I win a writing competition of 500 ink pens.

work to that of other participants. With no social media or online updates like we have today, the only way to find out the winner was to buy the newspaper daily and hope to spot the announcement. For a Form Five student, purchasing a newspaper daily was a near-impossible luxury.

The results must have been announced within a month, but I missed it. No one informed me of the outcome, and no letters, calls, or visits followed. As time stretched on, I forgot about the whole competition altogether. By July, I was convinced the prize had gone to someone else, and if I had won, surely the organizers would have tracked me down. With my name and school listed in my entry, it seemed logical that they would reach out. But silence prevailed, and I moved on.

One ordinary break time, my sister's friend, a Form Three student at our school, went to buy some snacks from a nearby vendor. The seller, who fried cassava pieces in a sizzling pan of oil, often wrapped the hot snacks in old newspapers. That day, the vendor happened to tear a piece of the *New Vision* from the previous months. As my sister's friend unwrapped her cassava, something caught her eye—our school's name printed boldly at the bottom of an article. Curious, she examined the paper more closely and, to her astonishment, saw my name printed right there! The long-forgotten competition had resurfaced in the most unexpected way, tucked inside the greasy folds of a humble snack wrapper.

It was about my winning of the five hundred nice clear pens that had been in the news for about four months, and there

I win a writing competition of 500 ink pens.

was no way I would have known about it. After being shocked by the article that featured my essay published in the New Vision, along with the announcement of my victory, she bolted off to find my sister and share the exciting news. My sister, equally stunned and thrilled, wasted no time rushing to find me with the precious piece of newspaper in hand.

I was in my class shortly after break time, and the lesson hadn't yet begun when I glanced toward the door and saw my sister beckoning me urgently. Curious and slightly puzzled, I walked over. We stood in the compound as she handed me the crumpled, oil-stained piece of newspaper. My eyes widened as I read the article word for word, an overwhelming sense of joy washing over emit was like discovering a hidden treasure — a miracle unfolding right before my eyes!

Yet as excitement bubbled inside me, a troubling thought lingered — were my pens still at the New Vision offices? Had they given up on me? Determined to find out, I hurried to the headmaster's office. Mr. Armstrong Kalinzi, our headmaster at the time, was astounded as I showed him the article and explained everything. Amazed by the remarkable turn of events, he immediately granted me permission to visit the New Vision offices and claim my prize.

When I arrived at the New Vision headquarters, they introduced me to the editor-in-chief. He greeted me with a warm smile and congratulated me enthusiastically. To my immense relief, he assured me that my pens were still in their

I win a writing competition of 500 ink pens.

storage room—they had been holding onto them, waiting for me to appear. "We were ready to wait till the end of time," he joked. The staff promptly arranged a photo session, where I proudly held all ten boxes of pens—each containing fifty—as they captured the moment for the next day's newspaper.

With my prized pens in hand, I returned home jubilantly, storing them safely in my room. The following day, I brought one full box and a few extra pens back to school. The box became my tithe — a token of gratitude to God — and I joyfully distributed some pens among my peers. I had acquired pens that would last me a long while, and my heart overflowed with gratitude. It wasn't just about the pens; it was a testimony of divine intervention — God's hand had not only enabled me to win but also ensured the good news reached me against all odds. The doors of winning had been flung wide open, and I stepped forward with new-found confidence.

Chapter 9

The Tough BBC Swahili Competition

In the year 2006, towards the end of the year, I was about to sit my final exams for advanced level, as it was a very tough time; the volumes I had to cover in order to be at a higher advantage of passing with flying colors were extremely overwhelming given the combination of subjects that I was offering, Physics, Economics, Mathematics and French all making a total of eleven different segments or papers as we used to call them not forgetting General Paper the twelfth. The only teachers I sincerely had were for seven of them, which meant that the five papers were to be done by personal research. The content was overwhelmingly vast. There was no way a lazy person, no matter how bright, could succeed in such a school—one that specialized in the arts—while pursuing a science combination! It was a ridiculous experience that I always remember and muse about the goodness of God and the boldness that he gives those that trust him. The exams were around the corner and we were studying round the clock at the beginning of October when the unthinkable happened! My father passed on! I was staying in town while he was staying in the village about 150km away. He had called my phone the previous day and I had failed to answer as I was in class yet I tried calling back and his wasn't going through due to network failures and I thought I would get another chance later to call him but it never happened. He wasn't doing well health-wise and I only suspect he wanted to tell me something very important yet unfortunately, I will never live to know what it was he wanted to say. Due to the very busy study schedule that we had at the moment and having heard nothing serious about his health, I didn't really make a serious effort to find out why he had tried calling and after all, there were other numbers he would call, and there was meant to be another time, I thought to myself. When I was informed of his passing, I couldn't believe it! It felt as though it had happened in another world, not ours. How I wished I had answered that call, and maybe I had tried much harder to call him back! There were milliards of questions that I could not answer, as I turned to God yet He was very silent. My world had crumbled and many expectations I had about my father's ministry had been dashed under the foot. Somehow, I thought for the first time that God was mistaken! Something wasn't right at all as my father had given himself into ministry all his life and he had walked with God. He had given so much sacrifice that he was our role model. He had survived too much to die at such a time before seeing the great ministry that he always spoke about. Moreover, at a time I was expecting to fight one of my biggest academic battles.

We travelled to the village for the burial and bid him farewell but my heart was extremely shattered with hopelessness especially in ministry. I had only a few days left before my final exams, and it took immense psychological effort to gather myself and focus on studying. No one was going to sponsor me at the university the same way it was impossible for my parents to pay my fees at that level. University was ten times as much cost as was advanced level and my only hope was in obtaining good grades that would enable me acquire a government sponsorship. We sat for exams finally and it was the stiffest year of exams in the history of Uganda National Exams as records tell, because the failure rate was highest on record as this was attributed to a grossly failed attempt of students' cartels to leak the right papers among students before exams. It was alleged that the examination board that very year changed their tactics and were fiercely fighting the leakage of exams among students by making about three different exam sheets of the same subject paper, such that at the time of releasing the exams, if it had been discovered that exam sheet A had leaked, then B would be dispatched. Most students bought papers at the last minute and concentrated on those very papers in hope that they were going to pass only to find a different exam with very different questions on the exam sheet! Throughout the exam period, many students

The Tough BBC Swahili Competition

came out nearly in tears, but my experience was different. I had prepared well and was not involved in any cheating. Moreover, in all subjects, I had done my best and despite the heartbreak I experienced towards the exams of the terrible loss of my dear father, I was prepared enough to answer the exams and pass with flying colors. In January 2007, while at home in Makindye, we used to sleep in the same room with my brother who is my follower and whom we had been with in Nairobi in the Church which my mother had started there. We both know Swahili, because of our stay in there for about five years, and knowing the language, he was an avid listener of BBC Swahili news everyday at 6:30Pm EAT on "*Idhaa ya Kiswahili ya BBC*" which refers to the BBC Swahili Service and the news program known as "*Dira ya Dunia*" (View of the World). BBC Swahili Service was planning to celebrate fifty years of Service in June that year in style and they proposed Swahili business-plan writing competition in which the winner would earn $2000 USD and a brand new laptop to enable him or her start a business and the announcement was running before and after the news cast at 6:30pm every day. Our room, once a garage for our late father's cars when we were younger, had been converted into an extension of the house. It was divided by curtains into two chambers—one for me and the other for my brother. Whenever he turned on his radio, I would listen to the news, even if I was busy reading or revising my books. During the vacation, I heard the advertisement on his radio. A thought struck me: *I could*

The Tough BBC Swahili Competition

actually win this competition! Without hesitation, I grabbed a pen and paper and began drafting a business plan for a candle-making business. What surprised me was that I was writing it all in English.

I had completed the business plan and was about to send it through the post when a thought struck me: since this was a Swahili station, the plan needed to be in Swahili. I carefully translated it but then faced a dilemma—how would I afford to send it to Nairobi? I had no money at all. As I wondered where I could get the funds, an aunt, my late father's youngest sister, happened to be passing by our home. She had missed my father's funeral three months earlier, and as she passed through, she stopped by to offer her condolences. In a hurry, she stayed outside, and I was the only one available to answer her call from the front yard. She handed me Ush 5000 as a consolation for the loss of my father, which felt like a great miracle and a sign of victory. I needed only Ush 2000 to buy stamps for the post office and send my business plan to the BBC office in Nairobi. This timely miracle seemed like a sign from God that He was involved in this. After mailing the plan, I returned to my daily routine and soon forgot about the whole thing.

Then, in March, my Form Six results were released. My mother went to pick them up, and while at the school, she called to tell me I had scored 13 points! It was a good score: three points in each of the four subjects, plus a distinction in General Paper, which earned me one more point. My friend,

The Tough BBC Swahili Competition

who had been revising with me at a larger school in Kibuli, scored only 10 points. While the exams had been the toughest ever, my score was considered highly commendable. However, I needed at least 18-19 points for a science combination or 24 points for an arts combination to secure government sponsorship. I cried like a baby upon hearing the news because it meant my chances of continuing to university had been dashed. I prayed and asked God for answers, but He was silent. No one could pay my fees, and I had failed to qualify for sponsorship.

My mother encouraged me greatly, and over time, I regained hope and strength to move forward. In April, as I continued life during my vacation as an English teacher at a secondary school, I received a phone call from London. A voice on the other end spoke to me in Swahili. The caller introduced himself as Solomon Mugera from BBC. I would later learn that he headed the BBC Swahili Service in London and had pioneered the "Faidika na BBC" competition, which was to be part of the BBC Swahili Service's 50th anniversary celebration in Dar-es-Salaam.

He told me that my business plan had been selected among the top four out of approximately 10,000 entries. The judges had first eliminated 5,000, then narrowed it down to a dozen, and from there, they chose the final four—and mine was among them. I could hardly believe my ears. For the first time, I knew that God had remembered me. Solomon also advised me to have my passport ready because the finals would take

The Tough BBC Swahili Competition

place in Dar-es-Salaam in June, where I would present my plan before judges. BBC would cover my airfare and hotel accommodation in a five-star hotel in Dar-es-Salaam.

I shared this incredible news with my mother, and together we set aside time for prayer, asking God to bless the upcoming event and help me win the competition. On the day we prayed, we stood in the front yard. My mother sat on the steps of the veranda while I walked toward the fence, praying aloud. After only a few minutes, she called me over. She said that a voice had spoken to her clearly, saying, "It is finished." We both understood that God had already made a way, but it felt too good to be true. I felt undeserving of such grace, especially after all the heartbreaks I had experienced. Still, I knew that God had worked through this.

In May, I received another call from London. They told me to ensure my passport was ready. Within the same month, I got my passport and was connected with Ali Mutaasa from BBC Kampala, who would travel with me to Dar-es-Salaam.

As I took my turn to approach the podium, the weight of the moment sank in. I looked out at the sea of distinguished faces in the audience—the President of Tanzania, high-ranking Commonwealth officials, BBC executives, media representatives from all over East Africa, and dignitaries from around the globe. The anticipation in the air was palpable. My heart raced as I walked to the front, the spotlight on me, and I could feel the eyes of everyone in the room on me.

The Tough BBC Swahili Competition

But there was something else—something powerful—that began to settle in. As I stood there, I felt a sense of calm, a quiet confidence that can only come from a deep place of trust. I had prayed, prepared, and practiced, and now I knew that I was ready to speak. I wasn't just speaking for myself; I was representing every single person back home who had believed in me, especially my mother, whose faith and encouragement had carried me through this journey.

I took the microphone and, without hesitation, began presenting my business plan in fluent Swahili. The words flowed effortlessly, and as I spoke, I could feel a connection with the audience. I shared the vision I had for my candle-making business—the concept, the goals, and the potential for growth. The more I spoke, the more I felt an inner peace, as though I was no longer just a young man standing on a stage, but someone who had been destined for this moment.

With every passing second, I could sense the judges and the audience leaning in, captivated by the clarity and passion with which I spoke. I felt as though the room had shrunk, and it was just me, the microphone, and the vision I had carried all this way. In that moment, it was clear to me that this was not just a competition. It was a divine opportunity.

As I finished my presentation, I couldn't help but feel a wave of gratitude wash over me. I had done my best, and I knew that, win or lose, I had already gained something invaluable—an experience that would stay with me for the rest of my life. The applause that followed was deafening, and

The Tough BBC Swahili Competition

as I returned to my seat, I could feel the eyes of the audience still on me, some even whispering in awe.

The judges deliberated for what felt like an eternity, and finally, it was time for the announcement. My heart pounded in my chest as I stood with the other contestants, waiting. When the host announced my name as the winner of the Faidika na BBC competition, I couldn't believe it. A rush of emotions—joy, relief, and gratitude—flooded over me all at once. I had won!

Tears welled up in my eyes as I walked up to receive the prize, and as I stood there holding the award, I thought of my mother and the prayers she had offered. I thought of the aunt who had given me the money to send the business plan when I had nothing. I thought of every obstacle I had overcome and every person who had believed in me when I had doubted myself. Above all, I thought of God's grace that had brought me this far.

This was more than a competition win—it was a testimony of faith, hard work, and divine timing. It was a reminder that no matter the challenges we face, when we trust in God's plan and give our best, He will open doors that no man can close.

As I left the stage, I knew that this was only the beginning. The journey ahead was still long, but now, I had the confidence, the resources, and the unwavering belief that anything was possible. And in that moment, I realized that the true victory wasn't just in winning the competition, but in the transformation that had taken place within me.

Chapter 10

The miraculous travel to the UK.

Having triumphed in the prestigious BBC competition in Dar es Salaam, I stood in the spotlight, my achievement celebrated in the presence of numerous dignitaries, including the then President of Tanzania, H.E. Jakaya Mrisho Kikwete. The Commonwealth was also represented, actively preparing for the forthcoming Commonwealth Heads of Government Meeting (CHOGM), scheduled to take place in Kampala that November. As a prelude to CHOGM, they had planned a high-profile one-day Youth Business Conference in September at the Commonwealth Headquarters in London.

During the ceremony in Dar es Salaam, as speeches filled the grand hall, a representative from the Commonwealth took to the stage. His words carried the weight of opportunity—he extended a personal invitation for me to attend the London conference as a distinguished BBC award winner. It was an offer wrapped in prestige: British Airways would fly me across continents, with my hotel stay and all expenses

The miraculous travel to the UK.

covered by the Commonwealth, and my visa arranged by their office in London. My sole responsibility? To deliver my passport to the British High Commission in Uganda at Kamwokya, where the visa would be issued without a hitch. Between July and September, after my return from Dar es Salaam, I lived in a whirlwind of celebration and recognition. Within my family, I was hailed as a luminary; across my country, my name resonated with newfound fame. The anticipation of yet another international flight stirred within me—a journey to the United Kingdom, a land of promise and global networking. Journalists sought me out, eager to tell my story.

Then, on July 2, 2007, my success was emblazoned across the pages of the *Daily Monitor*. There it was, on page three: **"Ugandan Wins BBC Award."** Above it, in a bold red ribbon, the caption read: **"CONQUERING NEW AREAS."** Beneath, an excerpt captured my voice: *"Mr. Ssegawa advises the youth to learn Kiswahili because it will help them pursue their goals beyond Uganda's borders."* Reading the article, I was swept away by a surreal sense of pride—it was my story, yet it felt almost like a dream.

Days later, *The New Vision* also carried my story, though the *Daily Monitor*'s rendition carried more punch. I purchased multiple copies, safeguarding them as treasured keepsakes, mementos to show my children and grandchildren—a testimony of my journey with God. My story spread beyond print; online media houses, both local and international,

The miraculous travel to the UK.

echoed my triumph. BBC Swahili in London kept featuring me lives on *Idhaa ya Kiswahili*, their Swahili evening news. From their Kampala station at Ruth Towers, they connected me via live telephone broadcasts, amplifying my voice across borders.

As part of their commitment to nurturing talent, the BBC's London office initiated fully funded mentorship sessions at Makerere University Business School (MUBS), ensuring I maximized the impact of my prize money. Calls from prominent figures at the university soon followed, inviting me to speak at symposiums about my victory in the BBC business competition and my growing association with the Commonwealth.

Time flew, and soon, September 10, 2007—the date of the Youth Conference in London—drew near. A call came from the Commonwealth Headquarters in London, urging me to submit my passport to the British High Commission in Kampala immediately. Yet, I was told to hold off momentarily, as they needed to liaise with the High Commission first. Days passed, turning into weeks. When the long-awaited call finally arrived, it bore an alarming question: *"Have you submitted your passport?"*

I was stunned. It was their duty to notify me once all arrangements were in place, yet here we were, scrambling at the eleventh hour. The entire visa process had been delayed by a simple oversight, leaving us to rush through the procedures in the final week before my departure. To my

The miraculous travel to the UK.

surprise, I was required to pay the visa fees myself and submit my passport to an agency at Fang-Fang Hotel in Kampala, which would then deliver it to the High Commission.

On the morning of Tuesday, September 4, 2007, I submitted my passport, with my flight scheduled for Saturday 8th at 9 a.m. The official at the Commonwealth Headquarters in London assured me that she would personally follow up to ensure my visa was issued that very day. With confidence, I was told to return on Friday afternoon, September 7, to collect my passport—just hours before my departure.

That Friday afternoon, I arrived at Communications House with full assurance that my passport, stamped with the all-important visa, awaited me. A call from the Commonwealth office in London confirmed that the British High Commission in Kampala had processed my visa as requested, granting me passage to attend the Youth Conference.

The stage was set. London awaited.

Everything had been going according to plan—until it wasn't. Arriving at the agency that Friday afternoon, my heart pounded with anticipation. Any moment now, I would hold my passport in my hands, ready for my early morning flight to London. Then, the unthinkable happened. The agent at the desk scanned the returned passports, then looked up at me with an apologetic gaze. "Your passport isn't here."

The words hit me like a thunderbolt. My breath caught in my throat. I struggled to process what I had just heard. *Not here? What do you mean, not here?*

The miraculous travel to the UK.

To make matters worse, the British High Commissioner's office had already closed for the weekend—at 12 noon. It was now 2 p.m. There was no way to retrieve my passport until Monday. My flight was scheduled for Saturday morning. My heart sank. The weight of it all pressed down on me, and in that moment, there was nothing left to do but cry.

As if on cue, my phone rang. It was the lady from the Commonwealth office in London. She was calling to confirm that I had my passport and was ready to board my flight. My voice trembled as I broke the devastating news. She gasped in disbelief and promised to call the High Commissioner's office immediately. But the lines rang unanswered. The office was locked, the staff gone for the weekend, and to make things worse, no one in London had a single mobile contact for anyone at the Commissioner's office.

The minutes turned into hours as calls were made in desperation, but each attempt ended in frustration. Finally, I received the call that shattered every last hope.

"There's nothing we can do," the voice on the other end said. "We have to cancel everything."

My British Airways ticket was voided. The reservation at Tavistock Square Hotel in London was withdrawn. The dream I had worked so hard for was slipping through my fingers like grains of sand.

I walked home in a daze, tears streaming down my face. It felt like a cruel joke, a battle lost against invisible forces determined to keep me from this extraordinary opportunity.

The miraculous travel to the UK.

I had informed Mr. Ali Mutaasa from the BBC Kampala office about the crisis, and he had tirelessly followed up with the Commonwealth office in London. But each time he called, the answer was the same—no progress, no solution. By evening, the calls from London ceased. The final decision had been made.

I was not going to London.

Exhausted and emotionally drained, I collapsed into bed at 8 p.m., the weight of disappointment pressing down on me. I questioned everything. *How could this happen? Why had God allowed me to come so close, only to have it all slip away?*

But just when all hope seemed lost, a flicker of light emerged from the darkness.

At around 10 p.m., my phone rang. It was Mr. Ali Mutaasa. His voice carried a glimmer of excitement. He had just spoken with a journalist who worked with the High Commissioner's office. By sheer providence, this journalist happened to be socializing that evening in a Kampala suburb—at the same venue as the High Commissioner himself. Seizing the moment, he approached the High Commissioner, explained my dire situation, and pleaded for an exception.

And miraculously, the High Commissioner agreed.

The journalist assured Mr. Mutaasa that by morning, my passport would be retrieved. I could hardly believe what I was hearing. My heart raced with cautious hope. *Was this real? Could this be happening?* I dared not celebrate yet. Even with

The miraculous travel to the UK.

my passport and visa, my flight was canceled, making the journey seem impossible.

The next morning, I awoke early, my emotions tangled between expectation and doubt. A friend, having heard about my predicament, dropped by to offer comfort. Together, we walked to an internet café to check my emails—since, at the time, mobile phones couldn't access the internet.

My inbox carried an email from the Commonwealth. They had arranged a conference call for me to participate in the London event remotely while remaining in Kampala. I stared at the screen, my heart sinking. *Was this it? Was this all that was left of my dream?*

Just as I was about to leave the café, my phone rang again.

It was Mr. Mutaasa. His voice brimmed with urgency.

"Your passport is here. And it has the visa!"

I nearly dropped my phone. My passport—retrieved! The impossible had happened! The High Commissioner had authorized his office to be opened that morning just for me. My heart pounded with overwhelming gratitude. But reality quickly set in—my flight had been canceled. *Was there still a way?*

Mr. Mutaasa, ever determined, told me he would contact the BBC office in the UK to see if they could fund a last-minute ticket for me to travel that very evening. I ran back home, barely able to contain my excitement, and shared the news with my family. They rejoiced, though doubt lingered in their eyes. *Could it still happen? Could the BBC pull off a miracle?*

The miraculous travel to the UK.

Without hesitation, I packed my bags. I refused to entertain the possibility of failure. I was going to London.

When I arrived at the BBC office in Kampala, Mr. Mutaasa was startled to see me with luggage. "You don't have a ticket yet," he reminded me.

"I know," I said, my voice firm with faith. "But I'm going."

With no confirmation yet, I had nowhere to go. I spent the afternoon wandering through town, eventually finding a quiet spot where people were watching a football match. Not being a fan of the game, I found a secluded corner, lay down, and tried to rest, my mind wrestling between hope and despair.

Then, at 4:30 p.m., my phone rang.

It was Mr. Mutaasa.

"The BBC has wired the money for your ticket. You're flying tonight!"

The floodgates of joy burst open. A miracle had unfolded before my very eyes. Racing to the airline office, I confirmed my flight details. Everything was set. By nightfall, I was at the airport, boarding a British Airways flight, defying the odds that had once seemed insurmountable.

As the plane soared into the night sky, I sat back in my seat, overwhelmed by the magnitude of what had just happened. I had stared defeat in the face, but God had made a way where there was none.

Upon arriving in London, I stepped into a new reality—one that had once seemed beyond my grasp. The towering

The miraculous travel to the UK.

buildings, the city's energy, and the warmth of the conference attendees exceeded all my dreams.

I had made it.

Against all odds, I had arrived.

The business youth conference was nothing short of extraordinary. I found myself in the company of brilliant young entrepreneurs, visionaries, and industry leaders from across the world. The energy in the room was electrifying—stories of resilience, groundbreaking ideas, and shared ambitions filled the air. Sitting among these inspiring individuals, I marveled at the journey that had brought me here. Only days ago, this moment had seemed impossible. Yet, here I was, not as a spectator but as a participant, a living testament to the power of faith and perseverance.

More than the conference itself, this experience became a profound lesson in resilience. It was proof that obstacles are merely stepping stones in disguise, that setbacks are just setups for something greater. It wasn't simply about attending an international event or meeting influential people—it was about proving to myself that faith, coupled with determination, could move mountains.

But the journey to London had not yet finished testing me.

That evening, I met with Mr. Mutaasa on the outskirts of Kampala, away from the city's congestion. From there, he would drive me to Entebbe Airport to catch a flight to London. With my heart pounding, I called home to share the good news: I was headed to the airport. I had no doubt in my mind:

The miraculous travel to the UK.

nothing would stop me now. Faith had proven its power, and hope burned brighter than ever.

But upon arrival at the airport, another challenge awaited.

"There are no direct flights to London until Monday," the airline official informed us.

The words stung, but I refused to be shaken. *There has to be a way.*

The only available route was through Nairobi. Kenya Airways had a flight departing from Jomo Kenyatta International Airport at 11:00 AM the following day. That meant I had to find my way to Nairobi—either by air or road—before morning. It seemed impossible, but I had learned by now that impossibility was just an illusion.

Two flights to Nairobi were available that night, but both were fully booked. The only option was to purchase a standby ticket for the 5:00 AM flight, hoping that a seat would open up at the last minute. I was also issued a confirmed ticket for the Nairobi-London leg of the journey.

Mr. Mutaasa suggested I return to Kampala to rest and then take a taxi back to the airport at 2:00 AM. I knew I couldn't risk it. Having already said my goodbyes, returning home would feel like retreating.

"Thank you for everything," I told him as I shook his hand. "I'll wait right here."

Therefore, I stayed.

The airport was a world of its own at night—dimly lit corridors, scattered travelers, the occasional announcements

The miraculous travel to the UK.

echoing through the hall. I kept my eyes on the departures board, praying for a miracle.

By 2:00 AM, the airport stirred to life again as passengers checked in for an Egypt Air flight. At 3:00 AM, my flight's boarding call began. My heart pounded as I approached the check-in counter, ticket in hand.

"I'm on the standby list," I told the agent, trying to keep my voice steady.

She checked the system, shaking her head. "You'll have to wait until all passengers have checked in."

Time stretched unbearably. I watched as passengers filed through the gates one by one, my fate hanging in the balance. Then, my phone rang.

It was Mr. Solomon Mugera from BBC Swahili in London—the man who had approved my ticket and was waiting to receive me at Heathrow Airport. Despite his demanding role as head of BBC Swahili, he had been following my every move, ensuring that I made it to London.

"Hand the phone to the check-in supervisor," he said firmly.

I obeyed, watching as the agent's expression shifted while listening to Mr. Mugera's voice on the other end. A few moments later, she handed the phone back to me and smiled.

"You're in," she said.

A wave of relief crashed over me. *Thank you, Lord!*

Forty-five minutes later, I was airborne, soaring towards Nairobi. When we landed, I had barely enough time to glimpse the Kenyan capital before boarding my connecting flight. At exactly 11:00 AM, the plane roared to life, lifting off towards London.

As we cruised above the clouds, I dialed home. My mother's voice trembled with emotion as I told her the battle was over—I was finally on my way to London.

Upon landing at Heathrow, another challenge awaited. Mr. Mugera had been delayed, and I had no British pounds to make a call. I turned to a kind passenger, explaining my situation, and they graciously handed me their phone. Within minutes, I was on the line with Mr. Mugera.

"I'm here," I said breathlessly.

"So am I," he replied. "Stay where you are. I'm coming."

Minutes later, he arrived and drove me to the hotel that the Commonwealth had originally booked for me. But when we reached the reception desk, another obstacle surfaced—the reservation had been canceled.

The only way I could check in was if Mr. Mugera provided his credit card as a guarantee until the Commonwealth reinstated the booking the next day. Without hesitation, he did exactly that.

I exhaled deeply as I finally stepped into my hotel room. After everything I had faced, I had made it.

The next morning, a taxi whisked me to the Commonwealth Headquarters for the Youth Conference. As I approached the entrance, the security guard scanned his list but couldn't find my name.

The miraculous travel to the UK.

"I was invited," I insisted. "Tell them David Ssegawa from Kampala is here."

He hesitated, then radioed inside. Seconds later, I heard an eruption of cheers from within.

"He made it!" someone shouted.

The doors swung open, and a wave of excitement and disbelief washed over me. My arrival was nothing short of a miracle. Delegates embraced me, their faces alight with joy. I had been counted out, but God had counted me in.

The conference was a resounding success. Beyond the formal sessions, I had the opportunity to explore London—its historic landmarks, bustling streets, and iconic sites. Each moment was a gift, a tangible reminder of God's faithfulness.

As I boarded my return flight to Kampala, I reflected on the journey. This was more than just a trip. It was a testimony.

A testimony that faith defies logic.

A testimony that God makes a way where there seems to be none.

A testimony that, no matter how impossible things may seem, if we hold on and trust in Him, *miracles will follow.*

Chapter 11

My Search for a life Partner

My search for a life partner began early, when I was still a young pastor in Nairobi, around the age of 23. Attending church, visiting neighborhoods, and socializing, I often found myself captivated by the beautiful Kikuyu girls I saw. I would imagine a life where I had a wife who truly cared for me, loved me, and cherished me, just as I would lavish her with my entire love and devotion. It was a powerful feeling, one filled with dreams and prayers, where I envisioned children who resembled me and looked up to me. The thought of building a family with someone who would share that journey was an exciting prospect.

However, searching for a suitable life partner was far from simple. I was in a foreign land, far from home, and had to decide whether I would marry a beautiful Kikuyu girl or find a fair and attractive Muganda woman from my homeland. The dilemma loomed large: how could I find a Muganda woman while living in Kenya, so far removed from my homeland? There were more questions than answers, and each one demanded a correct response.

My mother, who had helped establish the church where I was leading alongside my younger brother, resided back home in Uganda. Despite my outward appearance of self-sufficiency, resilience, and ambition, I was still young, physically active, and in a leadership position that brought its own challenges. As a result, temptations—especially those of fornication and immorality—were lurking around every corner.

Amidst this turmoil, my mother offered me counsel, emphasizing the importance of marrying within our tribe, the Baganda. She gave me a number of compelling reasons for this advice, which revolved around our shared cultural values—discipline, respect for elders, the roles of wives and husbands, and the way children were raised. She spoke of the foods we ate, the traditions we followed, and the societal norms that shaped our identity. Reflecting on her words, my mind began to shift, and I wrestled with the idea of marrying a woman from a different tribe, particularly the beautiful Kikuyu girls.

The core question haunted me: could I truly find the right woman in my home country, even while I was so far away? Would I rely on my family or friends to find her for me, and would they truly choose someone who matched my ideals? After all, this person would be my life partner, and I could not afford to make such an important decision lightly. Many of these thoughts left me feeling uncertain, and at times, I even considered disregarding my mother's advice entirely.

Meanwhile, I was living in a community where many young Kikuyu women, full of energy and beauty, were present. One day, a young Ugandan evangelist named Gershom, who lived not far from our neighborhood in Nairobi, sought me out after hearing that our church was being led by Ugandans. I was glad to meet him, and we spent many days sharing stories. One that particularly intrigued me was about his marriage to a Kikuyu woman in Kenya.

He described how, after three years of marriage, he came home one day to find the house empty. His wife had packed everything they owned into a truck and disappeared without a trace. This devastating experience shattered his life and his ministry, and he vowed never to marry a woman from that tribe or from a foreign country again. His story struck a chord with me, especially after hearing of similar experiences from others regarding tribal differences—how certain beliefs about children, wealth, and respect could lead to serious challenges in a marriage. The importance of my mother's advice about marrying within my tribe became clearer to me.

Meanwhile, the pressures of being a young, unmarried pastor mounted. I was meeting young women in the church, as well as married couples, and it began to feel as though I was imposing on others by offering advice without the experience of being a husband and father myself. I realized there was a whole dimension of life I had yet to explore—a life of marriage and family, which would ground me more deeply in ministry and make me a better-rounded servant to my congregation.

One day, my mother came to visit us in Nairobi from Kampala. She shared exciting news from the church she was leading back home: she had found a young, beautiful Muganda girl in the church who she believed would be a perfect match for me. I was thrilled at the prospect and eagerly awaited to see a photograph of the girl. I couldn't wait to travel to Kampala, meet her, and perhaps even begin the process of betrothal. As time passed, I prepared for the trip with growing hope that it would mark the start of something wonderful.

Little did I know that this visit to Kampala would mark the beginning of a new chapter in my life—one that would change everything. I thought I would return to Nairobi after a short stay, but destiny had other plans, and I soon realized that my life was taking an entirely new direction.

As soon as I arrived in Kampala, my thoughts were consumed with continuing my studies, and the idea of marrying didn't seem urgent at that time. Although I had met the girl my mother had mentioned, and noticed some qualities I wasn't fond of, I wondered if she had similarly reservations about me, which would explain her cold demeanor. Besides she was pursuing her secondary education and which I also decided to complete. Therefore, I decided not to pursue a relationship with her. Marriage, it seemed, was a distant thought, overshadowed by my academic goals. Still, the notion of finding a wife lingered at the back of my mind. I was back in my homeland, and I believed that, one day, I would meet the woman of my dreams—the one I would love with all my heart and soul unlike the girl my mother had found for me.

During my time at school, having joined in form five, I noticed a girl who captivated my heart. She was young, beautiful, and seemed to have a tender, kind heart. Known for her role as the chief dancer in the school's cultural children's choir, she traveled to many European and Western countries to perform and gain sponsorship for orphaned children in the school. She was admired for her grace, and her poise only added to her allure. Despite my focus on studies, I couldn't help but imagine her as my future wife.

Every time I saw her, my heart fluttered. I was shy, and I never found the courage to tell her how I felt. In her presence, I would feel like a young boy, unable to express the depth of my emotions. I loved being in class when she was around, and when she traveled with the choir, her absence left a deep void. Despite this, I never mustered the courage to confess my feelings.

From time to time, she would come to me for help with mathematics, a subject in which I excelled. I would always feel elated when she sought my assistance. But, despite the closeness we shared in those moments, I felt like she saw me as someone distant, while in my heart, I yearned to be much closer to her.

My Search for a Life Partner

As the months passed and we neared the end of the year, I finally gathered the courage to mention her to my mother. I wanted to know what she thought about this girl. Together, we devised a plan for my mother to visit the school without revealing her true intentions. She would discreetly summon the girl outside the class for a casual conversation, while my mother observed her, assessing her beauty and character to determine if she had the potential to be my future wife. It seemed unusual, but we believed that parents often had a special insight into a person's character that could not be easily seen by the younger generation.

On the day my mother arrived, it was just after lunchtime, and the teacher had not yet entered the class. My mother approached the classroom door, and with a quiet request, had the girl called out. The conversation was casual—about the cultural dance group—but in that brief encounter, my mother observed her carefully. I was filled with anticipation, eager to hear my mother's thoughts on the girl I was silently in love with.

Unfortunately, the news she returned with was not what I had hoped for. She told me the girl wasn't as beautiful as she had imagined, and in her opinion, she wasn't a suitable choice for a wife. She based her judgment on physical appearance, saying she preferred someone with fuller curves—larger hips and thighs. I was crushed. Yet, I knew there was little I could do, and over time, I began to distance myself from the girl. Soon after, rumors began circulating that she had been seeing other men while we were still in school. This only reinforced my decision, making me feel at peace with my mother's judgment.

As time passed, our lives took different paths, and we all moved forward in separate ways. Years later, I found myself once again searching for a wife while working at the Customer service helpline of a telecommunications company. I had joined the company after dropping out of university due to financial constraints. The helpline was an interesting place to work, where I often conversed with women whose voices were nothing short of angelic. Sometimes, these women would ask for my number, subtly trying to seduce me over the phone, but I never gave in. After all, these calls were recorded and evaluated, and I knew it would be highly unprofessional to give out my personal number.

On occasion, I would receive calls from female employees of the company who were checking on the performance of the call center advisors. These calls were sometimes tricky, requiring a great deal of care. Still, desperate to find a wife, I was drawn to some of the women I spoke with on the phone. One day, I decided to meet one of them in person. We arranged a time and place, and when we spoke on the phone, I discovered her expectations of me far exceeded my own. She likely assumed I was a wealthy young man, given my position in the company. People often believed that those working in such large organizations were well-off and more mature than they actually were.

My Search for a life Partner

You could see the disappointment on her face and mine too, being naive about how to handle women. I was willing to spend yet remained cold, and when I met her, I seemed like someone who just wanted to talk to her, and that was all. She was fair-looking but lacked the motivation to see me, and neither was I motivated. Right there, we parted ways, and neither of us followed up. I tried the same thing again. Having heard another very sweet voice, I expected this one to be a catch. While we spoke over the phone, she was kind and welcoming. We agreed on a time and place, a location near her home. After arriving, I called to let her know I had reached our meeting spot. As I waited, a nagging feeling inside me urged me to catch a glimpse of her before we officially met. I wanted to judge her facial beauty before deciding whether it was necessary to meet. I waited for her to notify me that she was approaching, and I stood somewhere she didn't know me so I could see her first.

To my shock, when I saw her from a distance, I could hardly believe my eyes! She had nothing on her face that was pleasant to look at. I could not afford to look into her face, as she apparently had some deformities that would make both of us shy to look directly into our eyes! I just turned and kept walking in a different direction, with no choice but to ignore her subsequent calls. I didn't know what to do next. I later got on the call, and I can't really remember how I managed to put her off, but I learned my lesson. The voice could hide the actual physical reality, and it would be hard to identify the right person from the helpline.

Around that time, my mother met a beautiful, kind, and humble young lady, but she was married. As they talked over some other matters, my mother was intrigued enough to ask if she had a younger sister who would be suitable for marriage to her first-born son—me. She suggested her sister, who was still in school, as a potential alternative. We made arrangements, and I met the girl. Indeed, she was beautiful, but through our journey of trying to know each other better, I realized she wasn't as kind and mature as her elder sister. I lost my interest in her, and after several visits to her school, bringing her many things, I saw she was selfishly after what I was giving her. I eventually gave up on the relationship.

The next time I was back in the search for a wife, I met a fellow colleague at the helpline in the telecommunications company. She was also searching for a man to marry. Apparently, her parents were demanding that she find someone, as her time to marry had advanced. She wasn't looking for a very rich man and was willing to build a life with someone serious about marriage. When I spoke to her about it, she seemed very open. In fact, she fell in love with me without me even realizing how she was feeling. As a born-again Christian, I had certain expectations for a partner. She, on the other hand, was Catholic, evident by the large wooden cross she kept in her drawer. She was aware that, in order for us to be compatible, she would need to convert to my faith. Before I knew it, she told me she wanted to convert to my faith and abandon her religion.

I was shocked at how fast things were progressing, and for the first time, I saw someone who was truly soft-hearted, humble, and down-to-earth—a potential wife. We could talk a lot at work, and our relationship became visible as close friends and potential couple. She even took me to visit a plot of land she had purchased, hoping that if we got married, we could build a house there. One day, I felt a hunger for prayer, and I went to the prayer mountain, a place I frequented once in a while for a few days. When I bid her farewell, we spoke, and she cried tears of love over the phone because she was going to miss me so much in the few days I would be away. I encouraged her that I would be coming back soon, but she shared with me later that as we spoke, tears were rolling down her face to the floor.

One day, while we were at work, she was putting her headphones back into the drawer as we were heading home. I noticed the large wooden cross in her drawer and asked why she kept it, especially since she had converted to my faith. She told me that she prayed to Padre Pio with that cross, and when I insisted we get rid of it, she hesitated. But her resolve quickly strengthened, and she confessed that she couldn't bear to part with it, saying she felt unable to live without it. I thought to myself that maybe she had come to my faith just as a disguise to marry me, but in her heart, she hadn't truly turned away from her religion. I had demanded in the first place that she should convert because I hadn't even wanted to propose to her. But here, I could see that, despite what she said, she wasn't ready to leave behind her religion.

I didn't mind it much, although it was a red flag for me. Every day, I found myself getting closer to making a decision to marry her, as I was gradually falling in love with her. She was simple, humble, hardworking, and, from what I could see, would be a faithful wife. However, she was a year older than me, which concerned me, but she had never been married and had no children. On the surface, she looked older than me, and I worried that, as women tend to mature faster than men, I could face difficulties if she outpaced me in the next decade. Still, I was struggling with the reality that I had been searching in vain for the right person, and gradually, I was falling in love with her as we became friends and cared for each other more every day.

She told me that she prayed to Padre Pio with that cross. When I insisted we get rid of it, she hesitated. But her resolve quickly strengthened, and she confessed that she couldn't bear to part with it, saying she felt unable to live without it. I was confused, yet my heart was drawn to her. My friend and his wife, with whom we spent the night, couldn't offer much advice because she was so friendly and jovial. The four of us had a wonderful time together. They made separate beds for us in the living room since their house didn't have many rooms. In the morning, we went our separate ways, but I still felt an overwhelming void that demanded a clear answer before it was too late. The negative feelings I had were stronger than the positive signals, and I felt like I was blindly heading down the wrong path, even though she was becoming more hopeful that our relationship was progressing toward marriage.

I invited her to join me on a trip to the prayer mountain, and she accepted. However, I didn't disclose my true intention: to seek God's guidance on our potential marriage. Once there, we spent time praying and conversing until late, when we separated to rest until the morning. I had brought an NIV Bible that my mother had given me, which I placed somewhere while praying alone in the men's wing later that night. When I finished praying, I searched everywhere for my Bible, but it was nowhere to be found! I had been to that place many times before without losing anything, and now I couldn't believe my cherished Bible had disappeared. I couldn't understand how it was gone. It felt like another red flag, and I couldn't dismiss it as anything but a sign from God that I was heading down the wrong path.

When I met my friend the next day, as we prepared to leave the prayer mountain, I was disheartened. She sensed that this might be another sign against our plans for marriage, and immediately suggested giving me her Bible to replace the one I had lost. I accepted it, trying to please her, but it didn't resonate with me the way mine did. The whole situation felt off, like a warning sign that something wasn't quite right. I made up my mind that I had to tell her the truth. I didn't want to waste her time, and being one year older than me was a sign that we might not make a good match. It was better not to deceive ourselves and risk hurting each other. She wept bitterly, and I felt terrible, but I knew I was doing the right thing for both of us, and eventually, she would understand. We remained friends because she was a mature person with understanding, and we continue to be friends to this day.

Afterward, I took some time to myself. There was no one nearby who seemed to be the right person for my future, but I kept searching. Every now and then, I would visit the prayer mountain again, asking God to guide me to the woman who would be the mother of my children forever. Meanwhile, I remained pure, keeping my motives straight, not seeking to use anyone sexually, whether those I dated or had relationships with. I was determined to do the right thing and wait patiently until God brought the right person into my life. A year after parting ways with my workmate, I noticed a beautiful, slender, light-skinned young lady in the mass choir at my home church. She was always at the front, very noticeable. Interestingly, she lived just three hundred meters from my home, though I didn't know that until one day, as I was walking home, I saw her walking and singing at the same time. I gathered the courage to approach her and greet her. She was equally excited, and we exchanged phone numbers, hoping to talk more in the future. Every time we met briefly at church, she wore a calm, humble smile. I wanted to tell her that I was interested in her and looking for a partner, but I hesitated. One Sunday afternoon, after attending church, I returned home intending to head to work that night. Feeling tired, I decided to take a short nap.

While asleep, I dreamt that I was seated in the back of the church service that had just ended, near the aisle. They invited this lady to the front to present a song, one of the songs she had produced as a music artist. In reality, she had indeed released an album of songs as an artist. In the dream, I could see her moving along the aisle, but she was accompanied by a man who escorted her to the front. I immediately thought to myself, upon recognizing the man with her, that she was already married, so I should not proceed with my plan of asking her into a relationship with marriage in mind. In fact, a friend of hers, one of the ministers at the church, had seen me talking to her and had tried to encourage me to pursue her, stating that she wasn't in any relationship and would make a wonderful wife. However, this contradicted what I had seen in the dream. The dream's message was clear, and as I contemplated giving up on my pursuit of her, another lady — a church minister who had heard about my attempt to befriend the choir member — approached me. She encouraged me to proceed with the relationship, assuring me that the lady had no husband and was earnestly trusting God for someone to marry her. This woman seemed to have no one to comfort her, relying on handouts from friends, church members, and a few sales of her music DVDs and concert earnings from singing at events with other Christian gospel artists. She didn't have any immediate family members in the area, so she was temporarily staying with a colleague from the choir.

I grew closer to her, partly out of a desire to know her better, but also out of sympathy for her apparent loneliness and lack of support. I needed more information about her life, and despite the dream warning me that she was already married, I continued to explore the situation to uncover the truth. I also began to interpret the dream differently, thinking that maybe someone else was destined to be her husband and that God was guiding me not to pursue marriage with her. Yet, despite my doubts, I felt a strong pull toward her, and I found myself caring for her deeply.

She, too, seemed proud that I was the man trying to build a relationship with her. Although I didn't have much money, I worked for a well-established, reputable telecommunications company in Uganda, and many young women would have been proud to be associated with me. Despite my reservations, I continued to move forward, and before I knew it, I was deeply entwined in her love.

As we spent more time together, I learned that she had two children from an earlier relationship with a man whom her aunt had forced her to marry. That marriage had turned out to be abusive and violent, and the children—who were around ten and nine at the time—had been left with relatives in the village. I began to understand the deep sadness and frustration in her eyes, coupled with a desperate desire for a new and better marriage to compensate for the love she had missed in her previous relationship. Despite my suspicions based on the dream, she assured me that she didn't have any man in her life.

I provided for her financially, as there was no direct support or stable income for her, and I felt it was my duty as a prospective husband to offer that support. As I continued to help her, I found myself captivated by the beauty in her eyes, which only drew me closer. During the day, when I wasn't working the night shift at the customer service helpline, I would often visit her at her place, conveniently just a short walk from my home, whenever her colleague was away at work.

As I got to know her better, I found myself on the verge of sin, tempted by the possibility of fornication as we spent time alone together in her house. I had mixed feelings—wondering whether she could truly be the wife I wanted from God, given the heavy burdens from her past, or if I was heading in the wrong direction. She wanted my care and comfort, and because of my sympathy for her and the growing love I felt, we would embrace, kiss, and hold each other, but we never engaged in sexual relations. This was due to her strong resistance, which I assumed stemmed from her faith in God and a desire to avoid sin.

Despite this, there were frequent instances when she would become annoyed with me over trivial matters, and she would retreat, refusing to answer my calls and even distancing herself from me for days or weeks. Yet, I remained hooked on her love.

We would often fall out over something trivial, and she wouldn't allow me to speak or engage in any discussion about it. Instead, she would keep her distance for some time. I would long for her love, knowing that she, too, craved mine, yet I had no choice but to wait. This on-and-off dynamic continued for nearly a year.

We eventually stopped meeting at her house because her colleague, who paid the rent and had authority over the place, had heard rumors from the neighbors about our frequent meetings in her absence. Her colleague warned her against inviting me over again. Initially, I was disappointed, but in hindsight, this turn of events proved to be a blessing in disguise. It helped us avoid the risk of tarnishing our reputation and, more importantly, the temptation to compromise our values.

One day, eager for us to spend time together, I invited her to meet me at a popular spot in the neighborhood—a large open space with tables and chairs, where people gathered to enjoy drinks, roasted meat, and snacks. I arrived early, choosing a spot where I could see the main entrance near the road. I watched as she stepped off a motorcycle and paid her fare. As I watched her from a distance, I noticed a few people milling about in the area. She began walking toward me along the walkway, but my attention was suddenly diverted. She wasn't alone; she was accompanied by a man, walking by her side.

Confusion and suspicion flooded my mind. Was she bringing someone to provoke me, or was she introducing him to me? They continued walking toward me, and my heart raced as I tried to make sense of what was happening. As they approached my table, the man suddenly realized she was coming to meet me and walked right past us. I was left dumbfounded and immediately asked her if she hadn't noticed the man walking beside her. She seemed unaware, likely focused on me as she walked.

We brushed off the stranger's presence. Apparently, he had hoped to catch her attention but had realized there was already someone waiting for her. Yet, the incident lingered in my thoughts, especially when combined with the dream I had seen earlier of her walking down the aisle with someone at church. Despite this, I dismissed any potential warning from the spirit realm and continued with the relationship.

A while later, a disagreement kept us apart for almost two months. During this time, some elders at church learned about our relationship and reported it to the Senior Pastor. One of the elders, a friend of mine, called me and shared exactly what the Senior Pastor had said. The Pastor, with his sharp spiritual insight, scolded the elders for not warning me against pursuing marriage with this lady, who he believed was much closer to the Pastor than I was. With his vast experience in life, the Pastor saw no potential for a successful marriage between us. He conveyed that she wasn't the wife God had destined for me, and that there was someone else out there for me, but not her.

Combining the Pastor's wisdom with the ongoing conflicts and separations in our relationship, I began to seriously consider ending things with her. However, the strong emotional bond that had developed between us kept me entangled. I was deeply in love with her and had become oblivious to the warning signs. Desperate for clarity, I sought a guiding answer from God.

So, I decided to retreat to a prayer mountain, fasting and praying for three days, hoping for clarity. On the third day, my spirit was finally opened to receive counsel. The dream I had seen at the beginning of our relationship resurfaced in my mind, and the Spirit of God revealed the truth to me. It became clear that she was not the wife God had prepared for me. The spiritual bond that had kept me connected to her was severed, and I felt free from her in that moment, while at the Prayer Mountain.

That bond had been so powerful, so painful to break, that I had been unable to move on. I would feel restless and lost whenever we were apart, torn between pride and the pain of missing each other. We'd pretend to keep our distance, refusing to acknowledge the depth of our longing for each other. Yet, inevitably, we'd find ourselves drawn back together, our reunion fueled by the accumulated hurt and yearning.

My Search for a life Partner

But from that moment on, the weight of that emotional entanglement was lifted, and I was able to find peace and direction, knowing that God had a different plan for my life. However, when I left the prayer mountain, I had been completely delivered from this entanglement. I knew deep within my spirit that it was time to move on. When I told her that our relationship was over, I didn't look back. For the first time, I felt no pain or hesitation about parting ways with her. Life continued as usual as I began my search for a future partner.

In the same church, as I became more active—occasionally interpreting for the junior preachers—I became more visible. My presence grew, and as a result, I caught the attention of many young ladies, some of whom I had no idea were even aware of me. It wasn't long before someone started gathering information about me and was determined to find a way to approach me. She was a close friend of a visiting pastor who regularly preached at our church. I had gotten to know him well, often serving as his interpreter during his sermons.

One day, the pastor and I spoke again, and he introduced me to the name of a lady I had never met. He assured me that she was hardworking, a nurse by profession, and a potential wife. He went so far as to give her my number. I met her shortly afterward at my workplace, and we began a relationship. She quickly began showing interest in me, bringing gifts to my workplace—everything from snacks to utensils and even clothes. She was eager and moving the relationship along at a fast pace.

As I got to know her more, I discovered that she had a daughter with a fellow interpreter from church. The situation was complicated—this interpreter was still very much involved in her life because of their child, but he was also looking to move on and had found another lady. It appeared that she was using me as a means to provoke him, sparking jealousy in the hopes that he would take notice of her supposed interest in someone new – namely, me. Chaos was quickly building, but even in the midst of this, I couldn't ignore the growing sense that she was not the one I had asked God for, nor the one I could see myself marrying.

Despite her admirable qualities - her tireless work ethic, patience, generosity, and empathetic nature - I couldn't shake the feeling that she wasn't the right fit for me. To make matters worse, she had tricked me into a sexual relationship, something I had always avoided up until that point. At first, she would visit my home daily to bring gifts, and at some point, we started spending time together in my room. I remember playing Christian love songs on my guitar for her, which moved her deeply—tears rolled down her face as she listened. Those intimate moments eventually led to us becoming sexually involved, something I had never anticipated.

She was very proactive and swift, even insisting that we both get tested for HIV, which she took care of financially. But as the relationship progressed, things began to feel off. She wanted me to meet her daughter and take me to meet her parents, but I hesitated. I began to sense that things were moving too fast, and I felt the need to pause and inquire about God's will before continuing any further. Although I had strong feelings for her, I was determined to make a decision about marriage that aligned with my life's purpose and values. I had seen too many people make irreversible mistakes, and I wasn't willing to risk making a choice I would regret for the rest of my life.

Realizing that I was resisting her attempts to move the relationship forward, she grew suspicious. I insisted that we enter a period of prayer and fasting for forty days, seeking God's guidance. That's when I started noticing how casual she was about our physical intimacy. Even when I tried to avoid serious consequences, like the possibility of pregnancy, she seemed to have a plan to manipulate me into getting her pregnant—just as had happened with the other interpreter.

At that point, I decided to stop accepting her gifts and asked her not to come to my house anymore. This deeply upset her, but I had made my decision. One evening, she asked to meet me at a popular spot where we used to sit, and she shockingly revealed that she had conceived during one of our encounters. I was completely taken aback. The news hit me like a ton of bricks, and I remembered a conversation I had with a friend at work. He had been deceived by a lady who claimed to be pregnant, but when he insisted on a pregnancy test, she refused. In that moment, I knew I had to think clearly and make a wise decision. I proposed that we visit a clinic to confirm the pregnancy, but she was vehemently against the idea.

It became clear to me that she was trying to trap me into this relationship, and I felt a deep sense of God's protection and guidance throughout this ordeal. Despite the confusion, I knew that God was helping me avoid being entangled in a relationship that was not meant to be. She refused to agree with me on taking the pregnancy test, and I began to sense that something was off. It became clear to me that I was holding onto a string of lies. In the midst of this conflict, I contacted the pastor who had introduced me to her. I demanded to know why he had done this to me, and our conversation quickly escalated into a bitter row. Our friendship dissolved, and I came to the conclusion that he was benefiting financially from this lady, which tainted his motives. He had connected us with a corrupted mindset.

When she completely rejected the idea of taking a pregnancy test, it was like a light bulb went off in my mind. As the truth dawned on me, I felt immense relief. I no longer felt trapped by the situation. With clarity, I vowed not to return to her or accept anything else from her. I knew I had to cut ties completely.

She later called me, furious, demanding that I return all the items she had bought for me. Without hesitation, I told her to come to my home, and I gathered everything of hers that was still there. I packed it up and handed it over to her. That was the end of our relationship. In that moment, I felt a weight lift off my shoulders, and I made a firm resolution never to engage in such a relationship again. I was emotionally and mentally exhausted.

From that point on, I withdrew into prayer. I kept returning to the prayer mountain, seeking God's guidance and asking Him to bring the woman of my dreams. I knew that the journey to finding the right person would require patience, wisdom, and divine direction. I refused to settle for anything less than God's best for my life. With an open heart, I looked to the future, knowing I needed God to guide me every step of the way.

Chapter 12

How I met the love of my life

Having gone through too much frustration with many ladies during my time of searching, I was exhausted and almost made up my mind to quit searching altogether. I resolved to focus on serving God and continuing with my normal routine work instead. I recall a pastor friend who was courting at the time. We were collaborating on some organizational projects, and I would often join him at his home during the day to work together. One day, while we were busy with our work, his fiancée visited him in preparation for their forthcoming introduction ceremony and wedding. I will never forget that moment because of the question he asked me: "When do you expect to get married?"

It was the year 2010, and though my wedding eventually took place in 2013, at that moment, marriage felt like an impossible dream. I was desperately alone and had lost all hope. His question seemed like a far-fetched thought to me, and I simply answered, "God alone knows." Yet, that question

How I met the love of my life

lingered, haunting me due to the deep frustration I felt in my search for a life partner. I had faced so much disappointment that I felt I could no longer muster the strength to search again. The entire process felt like a mountain too high to climb, yet I kept it before God in prayer.

One day, I remember vividly when I decided to visit the prayer mountain, determined to pour out my heart to God about my struggles with finding a wife. As was my custom at the prayer mountain, I first took some time to sleep in order to calm my mind and regain strength after accumulating so much fatigue and frustration. I knew that resting first would help me pray more effectively.

Towards midnight, I woke up from the men's chambers located in the men's wing, ready to begin my prayer. I went out to my usual spot in a large, bushy thicket with trees and scattered pockets of small trees. In the distance, I could hear the muffled sounds of others praying in their own secluded areas. I began to pray, and for hours I wrestled in prayer, pouring out my heart to the Lord and crying out desperately for Him to open a door for me to find a wife.

I remember very well that around four in the morning, it started to rain. Most people who had been praying in the thicket ran for shelter, but I remained steadfast. I insisted on staying, standing under the tree canopies that barely shielded me from the rain. As the downpour intensified, I became soaked from head to toe, yet I kept praying with fervor. My desperation intensified, and I made a resolute declaration within myself: "It's now or never! The Lord must intervene and bring me my wife."

By the time the rain subsided and morning dawned, I felt a deep assurance that God had heard my cry. My heart was overjoyed, and I knew without a doubt that God was taking care of my concern for a wife. That moment filled me with peace and confidence that my long wait was finally about to end.

I continued with my normal life, but my attention was completely diverted from the search for a wife, as though that was no longer an issue in my domain anymore. I continued serving God at the same church and working at the same telecommunications company, but I was confident that the Lord was working things out behind the scenes.

One day, a preacher from Tanzania visited our church, and he could only speak Swahili. Since there was no one available to interpret his message into English or Luganda, I stepped in. It was a chance for me to shine, and I felt so happy that in the whole church, I was the only person who understood Swahili well enough to interpret. Later, after some months, while I was in church one Sunday morning during the first session, someone called me to go to the office of one of the associate pastors. There, I met with a visiting preacher from Congo-Kinshasa who could only speak Swahili as well. I was scheduled to interpret for him in the evening service, and so we made the necessary arrangements.

How I met the love of my life

That evening's service was powerful, and I interpreted him with such accuracy and flow that afterward, he told me he had never had such a good interpreter during his time in Uganda. He asked me to accompany him to various churches where he had been invited to minister. I eagerly accepted, as I was always yearning to serve God at every opportunity. For some time, I moved with him to different churches, interpreting his messages in evening services after work or before going to my night shift.

After some time, the Congolese preacher was invited to a church conference about ten kilometers from our church. The conference was set to gather members from various churches, and this took place toward the end of the third quarter of the year 2011. I accompanied him to interpret, and that service was incredibly powerful as we ministered to the saints. During his sermon, the preacher gave an example involving a young lady whom he called out of the congregation. He referred to her as "Jolie," meaning "Pretty" in French, and shared a remarkable true story about a girl from Congo who bore the same name.

The preacher had a prophetic ability, and little did I know that the same girl he had called out of the congregation to demonstrate his message was going to become my wife! Apparently, he had seen her as a pure, precious jewel and had identified her as a potential wife for himself. He desired to use her to illustrate his point about the girl named Jolie, but I didn't pay much attention to it. My mind was fully focused

How I met the love of my life

on my role as an interpreter, and once my task was complete, I intended to leave.

At the end of the service, the preacher connected with the lady, obtained her phone number, and initiated communication with her. Later, he confided in me that he wanted to marry that lady and had even begun taking steps to pursue courtship with her.

I was suspicious about his move because I didn't expect him to be without a relationship back home, let alone a wife or children. I didn't ask him directly, but I wondered if the lady had taken the time to find out what kind of person he truly was and whether he was genuine enough. After some time, the lady, who had been searching for my phone number to inquire about this man of God, finally called me. She believed I had better information about the preacher from Congo. Yet, regardless of whether I had any information or not, I wouldn't divulge sensitive or negative details about the man I interpreted. Instead, I encouraged her to either investigate from a reliable source — which she didn't have at the time — or to seek God in prayer for revelation.

Indeed, she called me desperately seeking information about the preacher, but I had no details to offer, though I was highly suspicious of foul play. The preacher's relationship with her was progressing rapidly; he had already visited her home and was frequently meeting her in various social spots around town. I chose to ignore what was happening, but as their engagement advanced, the preacher began sending goods

How I met the love of my life

from Kampala to Kinshasa by plane, involving the lady in the transactions. Apparently, he wanted to do business with her. Due to the language barrier between the preacher and the lady, as their business discussions required more in-depth communication than their limited English allowed, she frequently needed my assistance, particularly when conflicts arose during their transactions.

On two occasions, she called me to help resolve some misunderstandings, but the preacher began to see me as a threat. He sensed that my advantage in language and knowledge put me in a stronger position. Additionally, the lady admired me more than the Congolese preacher and even preferred me to him, though I remained silent. I couldn't interfere with the man I interpreted or attempt to win the lady away from him. My heart was pure, and I didn't want to mix my integrity with any claims or misunderstandings.

However, the Congolese preacher eventually became a substantial burden for the lady. He frequently borrowed money from her to buy goods for sale in Congo but failed to return any of it. Instead, he kept asking for more, leaving the lady weary and increasingly wary of his intentions. This became a huge red flag that the man was not genuine. Worse still, he once attempted to corner her into sexual relations at his residence. The lady fought him off vehemently, and neighbors had to intervene. This was yet another glaring signal that he was a hypocrite preacher with hidden intentions. Moreover, his relationship life back in Congo remained unclear, and all these warning signs became a loud voice urging the lady to end the relationship with this preacher.

When he traveled to Congo, he called the lady after selling the items he had carried, asking her to buy more and send them yet he had not sent her any money from the proceeds of the consignment he had taken! This was too much for the lady, who was on the verge of sending the items out of fear of losing a potential partner. I remember she called me on a Saturday evening, wanting my help to carry out the assignment regarding the items to be sent to Congo in town, and we agreed to meet on Sunday afternoon, probably after the church service.

She purposed to attend our church service on that Sunday and wanted to inform me about it so that we could move to town together immediately afterward. However, I was not answering my phone because I had accidentally left it at home. She came to our church expecting to see me in the multitude of people, but unfortunately, all through the service, she couldn't trace me, nor could she reach me by phone. After the church service, I went back home to find my phone with many missed calls from her. She had given up and was heading back to her home.

I immediately called her and apologized for not answering her calls, explaining that I had inadvertently left my phone at home. Her calmness touched me so much despite the disappointment I had caused her. I offered to meet her right away without waiting for lunch, and she turned back from going home and decided to meet me in town so we could carry out the task. While in my office with her as I worked on some documents on my computer, I watched her, and she watched me. None of us said anything, but I wondered how a Congolese preacher had managed to hook a beautiful young lady from our midst while we were searching and failing. After that, we left the office and returned to our respective homes.

During that time, the lady was having a rough time with the preacher, who was harassing her badly for delaying to send the consignment. Yet he was not sending her any money but demanding that she use her money alone to buy items and pay for their transportation. She innocently sent the items, but due to the rough time they had over the phone, she felt fed up with him and decided to tell him that their relationship was over.

I learned about their relationship ending a few days later when I wanted to establish if the goods had been sent successfully. I sympathized with her and felt that she was in pain from the disappointment, but at least she had jumped out of a potentially dangerous relationship. About a week later, after knowing that they had ended their relationship, I had woken up in the morning but was still lying in bed, thinking about her. I immediately called her and apologized for not answering her calls, explaining that I had inadvertently left my phone at home.

How I met the love of my life

Just within a couple of minutes, I went into a trance. I saw myself and my mother on the roadside, and the lady in question was across the road. My mother was telling me to cross the road and go towards her! The trance ended there, and I came back to my senses, shocked that I had experienced a trance so suddenly and without even asking God about it! I felt extremely happy, and I could not believe how God was confirming my prayer and leading me to her in such a miraculous way!

I started thinking of how to approach her, and immediately a thought came to me to contact her elder sister, whose phone number was already in my phone-book. At one point, I had been sent by the Congolese preacher to minister at their church in his absence, and I had met her family. When I spoke to the eldest sister, she was happy to hear about my proposal to court their sister instead of the Congolese preacher, who had a significant age gap with her sister.

When she informed her about my proposal, she accepted immediately. The eldest sister conveyed the news of their acceptance, filling me with immense joy. When their mother, a pastor at their church who knew me well, heard about my proposal, she let out a loud, jubilant shout. My wife-to-be, who was in her room in quarters away from the main house, heard her mother's shout from the main house and asked what the noise was about. She was told it was the news of my proposal, which had reached her. Her mother had been praying about it and wondering why I hadn't proposed

How I met the love of my life

instead of the Congolese preacher, who was significantly older, had an unclear marital history, and was financially exploiting her daughter. Her prayer had been answered, and that day she rejoiced and even cooked a banquet for the family to celebrate the news. That was the beginning of the life-long journey of our blissful marriage with four beautiful children that is still flourishing twelve years now at the time of publishing this book.

www.ingramcontent.com/pod-product-compliance
Lightning Source LLC
Chambersburg PA
CBHW061729070526
44583CB00024B/3061